Jesus:

The

Corporate

Turnaround

Expert

Dr Michael Teng

Published in 2009 by
Corporate Turnaround Centre Pte Ltd.

Printed in Singapore
by Markono Print Media Pte Ltd.

9 8 7 6 5 4 3 2 1
09 10

Jesus, the greatest turnaround expert

Whenever you face challenges
Which are difficult to overcome
When the path becomes narrow
And treading it is no fun
When life gets you down
And motivation is lost
When darkness surrounds you
And you feel that all is lost
Seek out Jesus,
The all in one expert
The greatest turnaround specialist
Through ages come
Use His teachings to elevate
And motivate at least some.

Let Jesus be the guide
For problems that you hide
Just abide by the rules
And follow Him in an even stride.
Find the inner strength,
And face up to challenges.
Never ever fear,
The Master,
Is always here,
Right besides you
Holding your hand
Ready to guide you!.
So, Now! Seek out Jesus,

Jesus, The only expert
The greatest turnaround specialist
Through ages come
Use His teachings to elevate
Escalate and get the power
To differentiate, and motivate
You, my friend
Into the correct trend.

You can watch this video on www.youtube.com/1103teng

Table of Contents	Page No.

Table of Contents	

Background of the author

Dr Mike Teng is the author of a best-selling book *"Corporate Turnaround: Nursing a sick company back to health"*, in 2002 which is also translated into the Bahasa Indonesia. In 2006, he authored another book entitled, *"Corporate Wellness: 101 Principles in Turnaround and Transformation.*

He also published in 2007/2008/2009 eight management books, namely, entitled: *Internet Turnaround: The Use of Internet Marketing to Turnaround Companies*; *Training Manual: Corporate Turnaround and Transformation Methodology*; *Link Baiting to Improve Your Page Ranking on Search Engines* and *Corporate Turnaround: Global Perspective, Fundamentals of Buying and Selling of Companies, What we can Learn from the Animals on Office Politics, Turnaround Yourself* and *Corporate Wellness: Spiritual and Secular Principles in Corporate Turnaround and Transformation..*

Dr Teng is currently the Managing Director of Corporate Turnaround Centre Pte Ltd which provides corporate training and management advisory services. He has 28 years of experience in corporate turnaround, strategic planning and operational management responsibilities in the Asia Pacific. Of these, he held Chief Executive Officer's positions for 18 years in multi-national and publicly listed companies.

Dr Teng served as the Executive Council member for fourteen years and the last four years as the President of the Marketing Institute of Singapore (2000 – 2004), the national marketing association. Dr Teng holds a Doctor in Business Administration (DBA) from the University of South Australia, Master in Business Administration (MBA) and Bachelor in Mechanical Engineering (BEng) from the National University of Singapore. He is also a Professional Engineer (P Eng, Singapore), Chartered Engineer (C

4

Eng, UK) and Fellow Member of several prestigious professional institutes namely, Chartered Institute of Marketing (FCIM), Chartered Management Institute (FCMI), Institute of Mechanical Engineers (FIMechE), Marketing Institute of Singapore (FMIS), Institute of Electrical Engineers(FIEE)and Senior Member of Singapore Computer Society(SMSCS).

Foreword

Jesus is the greatest corporate turnaround expert ever. In addition, His manual for success is the most widely read text in history.

Therefore, in an age when corporations (and even the church) look to worldly models of success, it is refreshing to find a book that turns this on its head. Michael Teng reminds us that Jesus himself provides the tools to successfully turnaround ailing and dysfunctional corporations.

What provides a ray of hope to even the most dysfunctional of corporations is the fact that Jesus recruited some of the "least likely to succeed" and made them into a corporate dream team. In three short years, He "turned around" a motley crew into healthy, visionary, and productive disciples fully engaged in their corporate mission.

Jesus launched and still leads the world's most powerful and pervasive corporate entity in history-- the church; an enterprise that continues to expand and now has branches and customer service representatives in every nation on the planet. Today, hundreds of millions of "satisfied customers" testify to the positive influence of the world's greatest turnaround expert and CEO, Jesus the Messiah.

This book is laced with explosive spiritual insights that if applied, will do wonders for your corporation. Read it carefully and slowly and digest it fully. You will not be sorry.

Wayne Hilsden, Senior Pastor, King of Kings Community, Jerusalem Israel.

Preface

This book deals with a prolific corporate turnaround expert, who changed the course of world history during his lifetime and who continues to have an impact on the world today, more than twenty centuries later. His teachings are as relevant and applicable today as they were more than 2,000 years ago, and will continue to enlighten people as long as there are people to be enlightened. This man is Jesus of Nazareth.

Some have suggested that when looking through the history of human experience and behavior, there is really nothing new. Many historical religious texts, such as the Jewish Torah, the Christian Bible, Islam's Quran, and other works from Buddhism, Hinduism, and other world religions, show that people have interacted with one another and with the concept of religion in much the same way throughout time. In His approximately thirty-three years on earth, however, Jesus of Nazareth broke that mold and introduced concepts into the hearts and minds of humanity, which have a lasting effect and which persist to date. Jesus of Nazareth encouraged people to examine their own conscience and avoid judging others; He also spawned an alternative perspective on the way humanity exercised its faith and conducted it in the world. He taught principles like honesty, openness, diligence, and wisdom.

Jesus' principles are healthy strategies not only for individuals but also for corporate entities. He demonstrated that the only way to create change is to first change oneself, and then gradually change the circumstances that are within one's control. His teachings challenged humanity to abandon their self-made doctrines, which were unfruitful and contrary to God's natural order. He pointed out that the religious leaders of His day were leading their adherents astray, demanding that they live according to a set of distorted rules. These rules were often removed from the actual biblical principle and, instead, were merely traditions that had been established by religious leaders to give themselves the pre-eminence of being socially elite. Rather than extending charity and concern to the people they were committed to serve, the religious leaders had become like harsh rulers, wielding bitter judgments over those whom they were

7

supposed to serve. This gave people the impression that God was as harsh and vengeful against them as their enemies were. Distortions such as these, which can still be found in our world today, do not reflect the essence of what it was Jesus of Nazareth came to do.

Jesus, the first and only born Son of God, lived with humanity on earth for over thirty years as the paradoxical God-Man. One of His names is Emmanuel, which means "God with us". Within the divine plan of God to progressively reveal aspects of his nature to humanity, Jesus left His spiritual home in heaven to come into the world. The word of God which humanity had heard for so long became flesh in Jesus Christ so that humanity could now *see* the giver of the word. Once His teachings began however, Jesus became a rather unpopular figure with the religious leaders of the day, so much so that they successfully sought to have Him crucified. Much to their chagrin, however, this only strengthened the resolve of those who had embraced the poignant truth that Jesus had taught. Jesus prepared and commissioned humanity to continue His work, characterized by mutual love and respect for one another, and a love and respect for God.

Jesus' life on earth was lived sinless. Though He had come in the flesh, He willingly died a criminal's death so that those who believe in Him can have everlasting life. It is through Jesus that the power of God became available to humanity. Jesus provided humankind with a direct link to the blessings of God, and through Jesus, all can come into a life-changing relationship with the Father.

Jesus' death on the cross forever changed the way humanity perceived God. Through Christ, God is portrayed as the loving, benevolent Father who cares for His children so much that He gave His only begotten Son for humanity's sake. This event in human history was the greatest substantiation of God's love, the love of Jesus for all people. Jesus brought to the world the power of God to change the mind and heart of every individual who studies His teachings and truly repents, becoming baptized and therefore is reborn to a new way of life. Through this act, people are essentially reprogramming themselves from their old way of life, into the source of power, which offers not only eternal life in the end, but also a more abundant life in this world.

Jesus came so that you may have life and have it more abundantly. To study and apply His teachings can empower you to perceive what changes are necessary to establish a more fulfilling life as an individual, even as a member of a corporate unit. Jesus' work did not end 2000 years ago, but continues to this day and will continue into the future. He promised people 2000 years ago that they would no longer be alone. Though he no longer walks on earth in flesh and has returned to heaven, He sent His Spirit to dwell with us. It is through the Holy Spirit that Jesus continues to provide a source of power to all who submit and dedicate their lives to His teachings and ultimately to a spiritual relationship with Him. Jesus taught, healed, and performed miracles. He was the cornerstone that the builders rejected, yet He laid a solid foundation. He became the light of God's truth unto the world. He is still the source of power that is essential to establish a purposeful life in this world today.

So much more can be said about how Jesus' teachings have changed the world. Whether one is a Christian, Islamic, Buddhist, Jewish, a member of any other faith, or even operating with no religious faith at all, you cannot deny that since the birth of Jesus Christ, the world has taken a different course and has changed more dramatically in these past 2000 years than in all of its history prior to His birth. The self-proclaimed fact that His teachings can be adequately conveyed through the concept of "love" certainly has much to do with that. Jesus also taught that there were certain behaviors that would lead to failure while others would lead to success. These teachings will afford everyone who reads them a set of guidelines that, if followed, will empower them to find applicable solutions to everyday problems, whether at home or at the workplace. Jesus specifically spelled out methods of relating to one's workforce that is imperative to the successful operation of a business; accounting principles that strengthen economic standing; and management principles that pave the road to success. The goal of this book is to demonstrate the application of Jesus' philosophies to achieve the victorious turnaround of a business that is suffering and to strengthen one that is already flourishing. Whether you believe that Jesus was the long awaited Messiah, simply a great prophet, or just a great speaker, there is no way to overlook the lessons He had taught. These values are still applicable today and will continue to be so in the future. It is my hope that you will integrate these values in your life in your quest for success for they truly work!

9

Introduction

Jesus, through His teachings, has imparted important lessons of life that can be invaluable to managing our own businesses. During His time, he had merely twelve directors on His board, and because of His teachings and virtues, had converted them from humble origins to great characters, who are still acknowledged until today. They were not the wealthiest of men, or the most intelligent. Rather they were just fishermen, tax collectors, and yet Jesus had transformed them into excellent leaders. Indeed, God looks for ordinary men and women for extraordinary tasks.

Throughout history and to this date, the Christian faith has undergone persecutions. Governments from Roman leaders to communist regimes have tried to destroy it, yet the Christian faith came out stronger. Why is this so? This is because we knew that this battle is not amongst us but with the Lord. Therefore, it became the motivation of the missionaries and the evangelists to give up everything, even risking their lives to continue to spread the good Word to people. Without consciously knowing Jesus' contribution, especially in business industries, Jesus had endeared and changed their lives. Christianity is the testimony and the legacy of this empire that He has built.

Moreover, being a turnaround expert, Jesus taught many corporate leaders to be servants, incorporating ethical management principles with trust in God, thus enabling troubled businesses to become healthy.

Chapter 1 — Jesus and the Workplace

Many of the encounters between Jesus and other people occurred in the workplace. As such, Jesus' teachings provide many ideals that speak of the virtue of good, honest work.

Success in Biblical Perspective

In today's corporate life, most of us are experiencing a wakeup call. Everyone has a different perspective towards work, and career lives are excessively agitated, with no time for personal leisure. Men and women are looking forward to rewards, prestige, titles, and money from their companies. The dominating mindset is that career was more significant and important than our lives. These outcomes in the corporate world have jarred our concept and definition of success. Most people define success as an achievement of a specific goal. Success is having an objective and completing it, acquiring a "win" and not a "loss". In fact, success is found accomplishing much, in many areas.

In contrast, success, in the biblical perspective must be in relation to our purpose because in many ways, our purpose defines our objectives and the direction where we are going. Therefore, it is necessary that we must first define our purpose before defining success. Hence, the answer to the question, "What will make us successful?" will always boils down to "What is your purpose and vision in life?"

We must be serious minded in understanding our definitions and standards of success. We always wrestle with different issues and our importance in life is usually perceived with riches, work, and honor. One of the critical decisions we will be making in life is how we define success and which affects our definition of significance. This will definitely lead to a question, "Who becomes our definition of success and significance? Is it family, company, friends, ourselves, or our God?"

It is then of strategic importance to know our definition of success. It will always be determined by our purpose, which in turn becomes our source of motivation and value system that has the greater influence in the next generation to come. Our hope and motivation will always reflect on how we invest our lives. In

11

addition, our definition of success will always determine how well we value our lives, looking back on it in retrospect.

Maintaining Integrity through Honest Work

The corporate world is often filled with uncertainty and trepidation. In this fast-paced global market today, competition is fierce and often ruthless. Even at this time significant corporations all across the world are experiencing financial hardship and some are even closing their doors. Morality sometimes seems to be absent, or at the very most, lacking, in a world best described as 'dog eat dog'. Sometimes it may appear that dishonest people who are willing to tread callously on those who stand in their path are the only ones who are really getting ahead in the corporate world. This simple observation, however, should never serve as an excuse for conducting oneself without morals and honesty. Many highly successful businesses are operated by leaders who are grounded in Christian principles. Scriptures reveals that Jesus fully understood the need to earn one's keep in this world and that He promoted an honest work ethic. In fact, Jesus had a lot to say about work. Of the fifty-two parables recorded in the Scriptures, forty-five of them relate to work. In addition, out of the forty divine encounters listed in Acts, thirty-nine of these encounters occurred in the workplace.

Jesus once told His disciples a story about a dishonest manager. He concludes by saying that whoever can be trusted with very little can also be trusted with much and whoever is dishonest with very little will also be dishonest with much.

Be Guided......

Shake the dust off
Oh! you must
Because now you have a guide!
A guide! The Lord Himself
Is here to show you the light.
He's here walking by your side.

Remove the dirt from your shoes
Clean up the bad hues,

Purify the avenues
And move on!
In the midst of the
Muddy pond,
You cannot see the source,
Just recognize the force
And bow down. .
Let Him guide and help you
Realise,where the mud comes from
Let Him make the wrong, right;
Let it be a bright light!
Clean up the house,
Bring all things to order,
Let the love of the Lord guide you,
Into brightness,out of disorder.

Using Money Wisely and Avoiding Greed

What we have just read is only a short list of highly successful
corporations that have at the helm, a leader who is deeply
grounded with a faith in Jesus Christ. Their adherence to biblical
principles makes them well equipped to establish profitable
corporations. This empowers them to provide jobs to others,
support philanthropies that are dear to their hearts, and live a life
of abundance. Using their money wisely by reinvesting in their
companies, compensating their workers fairly, and reaching out
to the community to help others has allowed these entrepreneurs
to set a standard that others can look up to for inspiration.
However, the true inspiration is that of Jesus Christ, who
demonstrated by parables that to those who receive and use
money wisely, more will be given. Those who share with others
will receive more because of their generosity and those who look
after the best interest of the people and possessions in their
charge will be successful.. Those who are dedicated to their faith
in Jesus Christ are more likely to demonstrate loyalty to other
important responsibilities. Those who seek to follow biblical
principles in all that they do are less likely to fall into any kind of
wrongdoing (moral or legal) that will negatively affect their
business in the long run. Realizing that one is under the
watchful eye of God and longing to operate with integrity causes
people to assess their actions and their motives more carefully,

13

making them less likely to act rashly or too hastily. Avoiding trouble is better than overcoming trouble, and with God's guidance, trouble can be more easily averted. A famous billboard that has been depicted all over the internet intimates humorous messages that are supposed to be from God. One of them says, "Loved the wedding, invite me to the marriage". Applying this to the topic at hand, we could easily say, "Loved the business concept, invite me to the boardroom."

The Bible tells us that our Father in Heaven desires what is best for us; Jesus also conveyed this to His followers many times. It only makes sense that if we relinquish control of our corporate structures and practices to biblical principles that success will follow.

Management of Shareholders' Money

Sometimes we encounter the problem where there is an abundance of waste— where you order more of something than you need before it becomes obsolete, or perhaps you print handouts while in actual fact your co-workers can read the document if it is projected onto a screen during a meeting.

In this digital age, we are already able to operate in a more paperless environment, which can provide enormous financial savings in paper and printing costs. There are plenty of opportunities, even in finely tuned work environments, to find ways to reduce waste. Whether this waste is of tangible materials or time such as unnecessary motions or inefficiency, scrutiny will reveal areas where you can be more conservative, thereby saving time, effort, and money. Sometimes wastefulness can even involve a lack of appropriate activity otherwise known as a wasted opportunity.

Jesus talked about managing treasure wisely through the parable of the three men and their coins. The boss gave each of the men some money. The first subject took the money and invested it, generating a return that was ten times greater than his initial investment. The second subject did the same, generating five times his investment. However, the third was afraid that his master would be angry if he lost the money, so he buried the money into the ground until the master returned. When the time came to meet with his boss, this servant said that he knew his boss was harsh and he was afraid of his wrath, so he had protected the money instead of putting it at risk. This unwillingness to attempt to offer back more than he had received upset the master. Eventually the man was relieved of his money and it was given to the other man who had successfully invested the money entrusted to him. To waste an opportunity to invest what we have been given is as useless as throwing it away; knowing the truth means sharing it.

One of the most bemoaned negative impacts of money mismanagement is the current sub prime mortgage crisis in the United States. Many have failed and filed bankruptcy. A prominent case is New Century Financial Corporation (NCFC). NCFC was the second largest sub prime lender within the United States, and they took advantage of the government's lack of effective oversight of this sector of the mortgage industry. With the goal to generate more revenue from lending money to people through loans, they have overspent and have compromised the integrity of the company. As a result, NCFC is currently struggling for recovery. Furthermore, it is currently undergoing criminal investigations over accounting errors.

Respect for Stockholders

Another element that can damage operations in a large corporation is allowing disputes and disagreement to arise between the shareholders and management. There must be a sense of accord, or at least amicable communication between those holding the ownership papers and those managing the purse strings. Often, if there are not substantial earnings reflected in their dividends, shareholders will become dissatisfied and they will attempt to get to the root of the perceived problem. Sometimes that means debunking the CEO and installing someone who they believe to be a suitable replacement. Much of the time, this is a futile exercise in authority however, because the problems run deeper than simply the office of CEO. However, shareholders have the option to shake up the corporation and bring about changes that they believe are necessary. Sometimes a simple conflict that arises between the management and the board may turn into a melee where many are injured, sometimes irreparably. The best course of action is to maintain a harmonious relationship between the board of directors and the shareholders, with both groups working tirelessly to strive for the best interest of the company overall.

Consider the horrid consequences described by Jesus when the vinedressers (management) decide not only to ignore the needs of the owner of the vineyard (shareholders) but also to destroy the owner's claim to the vineyard. In this parable, a man purchased a vineyard and assigned a lease to a group of vinedressers. When the harvest was due, the owner of the vineyard sent for his share of the crop, but the leaseholders beat the representative and sent him away empty handed. Thereafter, the owner sent another servant who was also seriously wounded and forced to return to his master without the required portion of the fruit. At last, the owner sent his own son to retrieve what was rightfully his, but the leaseholders killed the son, believing that they had merely eliminated the heir of the vineyard. This, of course, enraged the owner of the vineyard, and he came and destroyed the wicked vinedressers, took back his possession and appointed others to tend his crops.

The implications of this parable can be clearly applied in managing a business owned by shareholders. While it is not desirable to have the shareholders overseeing every aspect of the company operations, when the time comes to provide them with the portion of the proceeds that rightfully belong to them, the management should not send them away empty handed or attempt to thwart the right they have to their funds. The management is accountable to those who own stocks in the corporation; and therefore, they should ensure that their dividends are provided to them at the proper time.

Also in this parable, the owner of the vineyard was clearly content in allowing the vinedressers to run the business, as they saw fit, never interfering at all. A group of shareholders will typically stay out of the daily functioning of a business but will certainly step in if their needs and rights are being abused. The turnaround expert who handled the case of the Enron Energy Company discovered that this huge multi-national energy company comprised of nearly 2000 companies—an absolute maze of

16

corporate intestines. It was one of the largest company troubles in the previous decade. This newsworthy case of mismanagement eventually led to criminal indictments at Enron Energy Company. The managers who were responsible for overseeing the best interest of the customers, the associates employed there, and ultimately the shareholders, were so busy reaping heavy profits that when the books were not up to par they decided to cook them. This dishonesty nearly destroyed a huge multi-national corporation and seriously injured most of those who became associated with the company by way of job or owning stock. Bringing in a corporate turnaround expert proved to be a vital move to restore solvency and renew trust in a virtual house of cards that fell exceedingly hard, all because a group of wicked vinedressers were determined to get their share of the crop whether anyone else got theirs or not.

Dishonesty and theft should be eliminated from any corporation to ensure the solvency and profitability of the business. There is simply no room to allow these elements to enter into any aspect of the business; and there is never any justification to warrant even a minor falsehood. Honesty and Perseverance are key elements to restructuring a suffering business or maintaining a healthy one. Solid communication between management, shareholders, employees, and customers will ensure the success of the business. Maintaining good communication is a form of love. We must interact with others using a degree of loving kindness that we ourselves would like to enjoy. Any broken link within this chain of interaction must be restored. It may be a meritorious endeavor to allow a corporate turnaround expert to come in and help a company identify where the broken link has occurred. There is no shame in asking for help, but there is considerable shame in allowing a business to fail for a lack of willingness to address critical issues. We go to experts for help with our illnesses. A struggling company is no different; it requires an experienced expert.

The entire world struggles with sin, disease, and degeneration. God sent the ultimate turnaround expert to assist us, His own son Jesus Christ. One of the names by which Jesus is known is "The Great Physician", because He healed so many who were sick, dying, and demon-possessed. He came into a sick world and left us better off because He taught us how to seek healing for ourselves and how to heal one another. By following His examples and His advice, we can enjoy life much more abundantly. Let us not be like those wicked vinedressers; let us be bright enough to cheerfully accept the generous help that has been provided to us all. Following the examples of the greatest turnaround expert of all times can help us in every endeavor of life.

Application of Biblical Standards to Corporate Endeavors

The title is not intended to imply that a business is a spiritual entity. A corporation does not have a soul. However those in authority will have to answer for the way they conduct themselves in operating their business. While a corporation is merely a means to generate income and provide jobs, products, and services, it develops a legacy that others will remember. Those who are in positions of authority can certainly attempt to adhere to biblical principles in running a business. They can apply the principles found in scripture that will enable them to find and take advantage of opportunities to provide better products and greater services. They can conduct the business lawfully, ethically and rationally, which will strengthen their standing with God and people. The officers of a corporation can strive to make good choices that are well informed and well thought out. The leaders of a corporation must choose to reject any kind of transgression that will certainly lead to degradation and decay.

Jesus was a different type of leader. He was a "servant leader". He did not think of Himself better than anyone else. He was willing to do the "dirty work" that others did not want to do and He demonstrated this numerous times. His service can clearly be seen when He was washing His disciples' feet and serving them at the supper shortly before He was arrested and eventually killed. Washing feet was the job of a servant, yet Jesus performed these tasks willingly to set an example. He was teaching His followers to serve others out of love. When you deeply care for someone, you want to help them in whatever way possible. While Jesus could have been waited on by many people, He came not be served but to serve. *He said that those who want to be great should first be servants.* Corporate owners can earn their employees' loyalty and

18

dedication if they first perform acts of kindness and think of the welfare of the people below them.

It is through the application of high moral standards that corporate directors become empowered to build a reliable and efficient company. Cheating, lying, stealing, and hiding material information, no matter how small, will have a negative impact on the business. On the other hand, honesty and integrity create a foundation for success. It is hard to have faith in oneself, and in others, if there are underlying devious schemes transpiring at the foundation of a business. It is truly said that there is no honor among thieves. However, a team of truthful, progressive, and loyal officers who are sincerely concerned with providing reliable service to the corporation will possess faith in each other. This faith is easily translated to action that will benefit the entire organization. Everyone connected with the corporation can trust that their best interests are taken into account. The shareholders will know that they can look forward to their dividends. The customers will be able to count on a reliable product or service. The creditors can trust that they will be suitably paid. Moreover, the employees will be able to trust that they will continue to have a job.

More than two thousand years ago, Jesus taught these virtues in parables that make as much sense today as they did when He first recited them. Honesty, loyalty, and faithfulness are vital characteristics for any truly successful person or organization. These characteristics create a solid foundation upon which to build.

Jesus explained that those who obey his teaching are persons who are building a house on solid rock. Those who do not obey are building their foundation on sinking sand, which will easily be flooded, blown over, and destroyed.

Surrender Your Troubles

Surrender, Surrender

To the Yoke of Jesus
As on the journey you alight
The burden will surely be light.
Surrender, Surrender
To the Word of the Lord
To the son of God
Surrender to the truth
Find some enlightenment!
Your life will achieve refinement.

Surrender, Surrender
To the hope, brought by Jesus,
Learn to navigate the path
From wilderness and treacherousness,
To reach out to the Lord,
And build a closer relationship
With Him- get adventurous!

Surrender, Surrender
To Jesus, the shepherd,
Savior of the human flock
The Holy one with humane feelings,
Who stands by all of us,
Never fleeing away.
Unto Jesus,
Entrust your life
 And get free of all strife,
That surround you
 Forever, In your life.

Successful Testimonials on Adhering to Biblical Principles

Many highly successful corporations have established their enterprises based on Biblical principles. One such corporation in the United States is Chick-fil-A, Inc., which is still headed by its original founder Truett Cathy. He and his brother Ben established their first business, The Dwarf Grill, in Atlanta, Georgia, in 1946. Through a keen business sense, their restaurant flourished and in 1967, Mr. Cathy opened the first Chick-fil-A Restaurant in Greenbriar Shopping Center in Atlanta. Since then, through franchising, Chick-fil-A celebrated its 60th anniversary with over 1,300 franchise operations in 37 States, plus Washington, DC. His company has enjoyed an unparallel 39 years of consecutive annual sales increases. One of their business policies is to remain closed on Sundays. This has been in effect since the business was established and there is no indication that the policy will ever change. The principle of "Sabbath" or of "rest" is at work here. *Quite simply, a rested staff is a more productive staff.* Interestingly enough the principle of "Sabbath" is a foundational Christian principle.

Cathy is a man of devout faith who strives to give back to the community. He has based his life and his business practices on biblical principles, philanthropy, and hard work. He commits his time and energy to community service and has taught a Sunday school class for 13-year-old boys for 50 years running. He said, *"Nearly every moment of every day, we have the opportunity to give something to someone else— our time, our love, our resources. I have always found more joy in giving when I did not expect anything in return".*

Cathy and his family developed and sponsored a variety of programs that aim at providing necessary community services. He is particularly passionate about attending to the needs of foster children through his WinShape® Foundation, founded and administrated together with his wife Jeanette. His children have also followed his footsteps, both running the corporation and committing themselves to programs that benefit their community. In addition, Chick-fil-A awards numerous scholarships to students attending Berry College in Atlanta. Cathy's family continuously finds new ways to give back to others. He was bestowed countless awards and has authored several books that are inspiring and compelling. At 85, Truett Cathy is still a very vibrant and inspiring man, dedicated to his faith in God and to his community.

Another highly successful American businessman, David Green, is the CEO and Founder of Hobby Lobby Creative Centers based in Oklahoma City, Oklahoma.

Commencing in 1972, Hobby Lobby was an outgrowth of Greco Products, Inc., also founded by David Green. From humble beginnings, this corporation has grown into a 1.8 billion dollar industry of 386 stores throughout 30 states within the United States. The company operates with the following statement of purpose:

To serve our owners, employees, and customers effectively, the Board of Directors is committed to:

Honoring the Lord in all we do by operating the company in a manner consistent with Biblical principles.

Offering our customers an exceptional value.

Serving our employees and their families by establishing a work environment and company policies that build character, strengthen individuals, and nurture families.

Providing a return on the owners' investment, sharing the Lord's blessings with our employees, and investing in our community.

Green's stores are also closed on Sundays and the corporation is involved in community outreach programs aimed at encouraging people through Scripture. Green believes that God's grace and provision has allowed Hobby Lobby to endure through the years.

Many of the wealthiest businesspersons in the United States are devout Christians, and have used biblical principles to establish and operate their corporations. In addition to those already mentioned, consider Phillip Anschultz, who owns several major sports teams, ranch lands, railroads, telecommunications companies, and movie theaters, just to name a few. He has a personal net worth of billions and also is has a passionate faith in Christ. Add to this list Bo Pilgrim, founder of Pilgrim's Pride, which is the second largest poultry producer in the United States, with exports of commodity chicken products to Russia, China, Japan, and Kazakhstan.

The Lamoiyan Corporation in the Philippines also operates in accordance with biblical principles. It is one of the leading manufacturers of toothpaste and dishwashing products in the country. Cecilio Pedro, Chief Executive Officer of the company, says that *they face challenges with an unwavering faith in God who inspires and guides all of their actions.*

Lamoiyan, like the company motto states, is committed to make a difference for the glory of God. Pedro does not only take care of the physical and intellectual well-being of his employees but their spiritual well-being as well. As a social responsibility, the company also employs the physically handicapped.

Key Learning Points:

o   Success is related to our purpose.
o   Whoever can be trusted with little, can also be trusted with much.
o   Manage company's treasure wisely.
o   Applications of Biblical standards bring success.

Chapter 2 — Engaging in a Turnaround Requires Understanding the Pitfalls

As success has been the motivation for the turnaround, the initial step is to understand the pitfalls in pursuing success in a wrong way. The prosperity of a business is hugely dependent on a good management. Good management sometimes needs to undergo certain turnaround, revision of policies, overhaul of systems and restructuring. In all of these, a cleanup in all corners of the corporation is necessary. There could be dust or sins that need to be swept out of the door of the business.

Compromise is Always Coupled with Consequence

Sometimes, an overview of our business will give us a perspective that seems a little murky. It is hard to discern how circumstances really look like because we are clouded by confusing issues and principles. When we continue to allow these issues to obstruct our views, they may lead us to sinfulness. In business, like life, the wages of sin is death. In the context of a business enterprise, this death may mean bankruptcy and shutting down.

A reconstruction and cleaning may be necessary to get real things back on the surface. If we are honest with ourselves, we can easily find elements in our business that need to be cleaned up— *inefficiencies that slow down productivity, wastefulness that drains away our resources, dishonesty that hinders our ability to address the issues* that need attention. Those clutters are sin and like a disease, it can denigrate everything it runs through. With proper treatment, one can get rid of the disease. This holds true for dispelling sin from everyday life.

It may seem to many people around the world, that the Americans have chosen differently this time in their election of President. The faith and trust that the common American man has shown in another common man from very humble beginnings has much to say about the current mindset of the American population . People want a young, sensible, action packed man, who is ready to do all to save his country. In the words of Barack

Obama, "Change will not come if we wait for some other person or some other time. We are the ones we've been waiting for. We are the change that we seek." With the election of Obama to the White House, Americans have found their Turnaround Expert, the CEO who can feel for them and can relate to their circumstances, fears and anxieties and find solutions for them.

Obama has been handed a messy platter of American crisis as soon as he took up office, which in his words is, "I found this national debt, doubled, wrapped in a big bow waiting for me as I stepped into the Oval Office." yet, he is confident in finding solutions to all the issues which ravage the world. He says, "This is the moment when we must come together to save this planet. Let us resolve that we will not leave our children a world where the oceans rise and famine spreads and terrible storms devastate our lands." He also remarked in one of his speeches that, "We need to steer clear of this poverty of ambition, where people want to drive fancy cars and wear nice clothes and live in nice apartments but don't want to work hard to accomplish these things. Everyone should try to realize their full potential."

The faith that millions have put into Obama by choosing him as their leader will definitely propel Obama to solve the crisis which is devastating his country. Barack Obama has a very difficult task cut out for him: to turnaround the economic crisis that has brought about the America to the brink of financial disaster. Barack Obama if he succeeds may yet go down in history as a great turnaround expert of the twenty first century.

Tens of thousands of people all across America are losing their jobs, struggling to pay the bills, facing foreclosure of the businesses and factories. This is why America needs a new and immediate economic recovery plan to get the country out of severe economic crisis.

In ancient practices of worship, people would offer a sacrificial animal or some other offering to 'cleanse' themselves from their sin. However, people had kept making the same mistakes and sinful acts and never achieved the sense of peace required to live a successful life. It was, in essence, a form of insanity. This kind of practice is unhealthy . Continuing to conduct a business in this manner may surely bring about the demise of the company. No amount of sacrificing will save a business that continues to perform errantly.

Since they believed that they will soon die as a consequence of being sinful, Jews in the Biblical times instituted a different way of cleansing themselves of sin. They elected to follow the teachings of John the Baptist, who instituted the practice of baptism. Baptism is a way of renouncing sin and washing away the effects of sin through water immersion. *In Christianity, the act of baptism is further associated with dying in the old ways of life, being cleansed and renewed to a new birth.* This action not only demonstrates one's belief that Jesus had willingly died for the sins of the world but also willingness to die as the person they were before and become a new person in Christ. Being renewed means beginning to follow Christian morals.

In the business organization, before cleaning up the problems and creating a new way of operation, it is necessary to renounce those sinful practices that make the business unclean, and therefore unsuccessful. The core of the business must be clean and efficient before expecting that all of the members will function correctly and efficiently. You must immerse your entire business in the cleansing waters of change in order to affect the necessary renewal that will empower your company.

Continuous conformity to sinful acts will eventually sacrifice the profitability of the company. You may be blinded by the sudden success in revenue increase but those unrighteous practices will bring the income down and affect the wholesomeness of the corporation.

Wastefulness Causes Want; Make Efficient Use of Assets

When you are standing in the middle of a muddy pond, you cannot see where the mud is coming from. However, an interested observer standing on the edge of the water, looking in can discern where the dirt originates and can point it out to you. You can then gain insights as to how to dam up the flow of the mud to restore the pond to its crystal clear, pristine condition that you desire.

Sometimes, being immersed deeply in the day-to-day operations of your business is overwhelming enough to cloud your views. When something wrong occurs, you may not be able to tell precisely where the problem lies. Other times, you may have an idea of what is wrong but it is simply hard to admit what the problems are until they have been pointed out and become undeniable. *It really helps to bring in the view of an objective outsider to see the causes of unclean business practices.* A corporate turnaround expert will be able to search in those places that you have overlooked because you were trying to deal with all the obvious chores. If you have been unwilling to face the problems of your business, the turnaround expert will turn you in the right direction to face your problems head on. Facing the causes is the only way to solve any problem. Once the issues are identified, you can classify the tools that will be necessary to accomplish the clean up effort. It is much like receiving a diagnosis for a physical illness; once you know what the sickness is, the right medicine can be prescribed.

Take the example of China. To showcase the country to the world, China has stepped into a quagmire of problems. For the Olympics, factories were shifted out of Beijing , water was shipped from surrounding provinces ,leaving the farms without water. The farmers were paid paltry sums of money to ship water to the capital city. Many factories were shut down to control the pollution levels. Domestically, the country suffered .The Olympic games turned out to be the beginning of economic and political disaster for the country.

Chinese economy is threatened by three factors: weakening global growth, severe weather conditions and high unemployment.

With the slowdown in the world economy, China is already facing crisis. The US sub prime crisis has caused ripples all over the world and with the volatile financial markets, the Chinese exports will be meager. Exports of inexpensive goods are the mainstay of the economy in China, which will be hard hit now.

Therefore, to move on to the next step, shaking off the dirt is necessary. When Jesus sent His apostles out to preach the Gospel, He instructed them to take nothing with them. They were to earn their keep in each town they visited, but Jesus said that when they enter a community they should find a place where they were welcomed. If no one in the town welcomed them, they were instructed to shake off the dirt from their sandals before moving on to the next place. Therefore, *when dust has made your business unclean, shake it off,* and then proceed in integrating the truth in your operations.

The most common unclean practices were alluded to earlier but they warrant closer examination. The first and most common are the inefficiencies in operations that slow down productivity. These are often related to a failure or unwillingness to abandon an antiquated way of doing business.

Some inefficiencies that are evident in many business organizations include a sales representative who can gather new orders in the field but stays in the office and hand-writes only a few; a machine that breaks down so often and your repair technician is not able to fix; and communicating with satellite offices by long distance calls while you can use E-mail or instant messaging.

A thorough examination of your own business operation will reveal to you what kinds of issues are draining your time, energy, and money. Efficiency could mean, sending your customer sales representatives to the field or letting them use the telephone to enlist new customers; buying a new machine to replace the erroneous one instead of paying a technician every time it breaks down; and cutting off your phone expenses while using a more convenient and cheaper way.

Sometimes it might be easier to just step aside and allow other experts to evaluate where the inefficiencies lie. Ford motor company did just that when they began to suffer financially in 2006. The CEO, who is a member of the Ford family, brought in a turnaround team to work out the dilemma that his organization was facing. These measures were well communicated to all the concerned parties such as the employees and shareholders; and the company experienced hardly any fluctuation in the listed share prices.

Gujarat Ambuja Cements Limited, third largest cement producer in India, trains its employees to be efficient through a work philosophy that has already worked for more than 20 years. It is simply, *"let people set their own targets, give them freedom to achieve them and their task becomes a personal mission: I Can."*

Its employees have learned how to be self-responsible and accountable to the works that are assigned to them. They have the urge to push their limits and help improve the services they can render to the company and the company to its clients.

Lying is a Deadly Sin

One factor that can do your business the most harm is dishonesty. This makes perfectly good sense when you consider that lying is a violation of one of God's commandments. Whether you have workers that are not living up to their responsibilities while attempting to look busy and productive; or you are denying issues that are causing an adverse effect on your bottom line, they must be addressed inspite of how painful it is for you to admit. If you are unable to pull orders or produce an order in four days, you should never promise your customer that it would ship in two days. Such things have a way of catching up with you and driving away potential income. *A simple truth in business: satisfied customers spread the word about your company to two or three people; while upset customers can share your defect with everyone they know.* They will even tell strangers on the street that your company unjustly treated them. Of course, no one would intentionally mistreat customers but it is easy to make them feel that you do not care about them if your orders consistently arrive later than expected, or you do not return their calls in a timely manner. You may not even see these things happening, but if you are having issues with customers, you can be sure that a corporate turnaround expert will see them, and will not hesitate to tell you what is causing customer displeasure.

Key Learning Points:

- Cleaning up the corporation needs the knowledge to remove dust and dirt from all of the corners.
- Even the smallest act of compromising has an equivalent consequence.
- Moving to the next step requires shaking of the dirt.
- Lying or dishonesty is against God's commandment and it could be of great harm to the business.

Chapter 3 — Defining Purpose and Goals: Critical Steps toward Turnaround

"You are the salt of the earth, but if the salt loses its flavor, how shall it be seasoned? It is then good for nothing but to be thrown out and trampled underfoot by men." Jesus Christ.   Matthew 5:13

Turn to Jesus for turnaround

Whatever your cross, whatever your pain,
Turn to the Lord, it'll never be in vain.
Whenever you need help,
Here's some sound advice
Turn only to Jesus.
Just turn to Jesus!
When the going is not good,
Just turn to Jesus!
Whenever you have to purify your heart,
Just turn to Jesus!

Jesus, the Turnaround Expert
Jesus, the Turnaround Expert
Jesus, the Turnaround Expert, of all times!

Jesus, who lived and died
To teach mankind,
About kindness and love
To be happy and wise,
To hold the head up and rise
No matter what the strife.
To help you make a turnaround
In your Corporate life!

Just follow the advice,
Of the Greatest Turnaround Expert
Jesus, Oh lord Jesus!
He was so very, very wise!
Turn to his teachings
Turn to his principles as guide,
Turn to his sacrifice

Because, Jesus is the Greatest,
The Greatest Turnaround Expert
Of all times!

If you follow The Path, guided by Jesus
You are sure to acquire
Your heart's every desire.
Nullify the falsehood,
Don't justify the queer
You don't have to follow your peer.
Remember the golden words of Jesus
"Never fear, for I am here!!"

Does your corporation or business operate around a well-defined vision, mission, and goals (VMG)? Do all your company structures adhere to the VMG, or some are already diverted to fulfill their own self-interests? Many successful businesses trace their prosperity to their clear VMG. VMG provides companies with clear path to travel, and transparent agreements of service and product delivery to their customers, wages and benefits to their employees, and revenues to their shareholders.

Define Your Purpose to Determine Your Direction

One frequently overlooked but crucial aspect of establishing or re-establishing a corporation is defining its purpose or redefining the initial purpose after conditions have changed. Many companies are struggling because they are not able to adapt to being competitive in a global marketplace. Sometimes a company may not be able to maintain a competitive edge unless it is willing to delegate some of the operations to others in the form of alliances.

Dell Corporation is a good example. After examining its position in the market and recruiting the help of turnaround experts, Dell made critical decisions that were based on their objective to maintain their status as a leading supplier of computer equipment. Dell has established itself as a forerunner in the industry of supplying top quality computers to private consumers and major corporations alike. They have done this, not by stubbornly insisting that they have to manufacture all the components that make up their product line but rather by collaborating with other suppliers who are able to manufacture components for them. They have formed alliances with vendors who are well prepared to design and create equipment that Dell are not able to make. This has enabled them to concentrate on the basic purpose of their business — offering direct sales of exceptional quality computer equipment and providing outstanding customer service.

Having a company's purpose clearly defined empowers the management to look outside of them and form alliances that are beneficial to all who are involved. This was the case with Minco Corporation, which needed to fulfill the needs of customized medical and aeronautic products in the Asia/Pacific marketplace. By forming an alliance with a corporation in Singapore, they were able to establish a design and service center in close proximity to their customers, which enabled them to continue to fulfill their purpose to be a leading provider of these products and build a loyal customer base in the Asia/Pacific region of the world.

Jesus was born with a clear and well-defined purpose. God had planned this since the beginning of humankind. Jesus came to fulfill the long awaited promise of a Savior to the descendants of Abraham. However, His purpose was so much greater than that- He reached far beyond Judea to provide salvation to Jews and Gentiles alike. His ministry has traveled worldwide to reach people even in the most remote parts of the world. He was a great teacher, instructing everyone around Him by way of thought provoking parables. He was also a healer to those who were sick, demonstrating great kindness and compassion. He set an example that his followers emulated. Thus, missionary ministries were established to feed the starving, offer medical care to the sick and provide housing to the poor. He made it clear, in no uncertain terms, that we should care for one another and help those who are less fortunate. He performed miracles in the sight of men and some who had faith in Him were healed simply by virtue of their faith. One woman sought Him out, but was afraid to approach Him, so she believed that if she could merely touch His robe she would be healed of her infirmary. He knew immediately that someone had received healing and turned to greet her, assuring her that her faith had healed her of her infirmary. A centurion in the Roman army asked Jesus to heal his servant, but indicated that he himself was not worthy that Jesus should visit his home. However, he believed it was not necessary for Jesus to even touch the servant to heal him, that he had only to speak it and it would be done. Jesus was deeply touched and impressed with the depth of faith that this request implied. As a result, the servant was indeed healed.

These days nearly every major corporation uses some form of executive training program. Executives are expected to understate the corporate vision, the company's code of ethics and the mission statement. Each of these elements specifically addresses the direction the company is attempting to follow. These elements, along with the expertise of a corporate turnaround expert to provide guidance and perspective, can bring about a much-needed change to the methods used to operate a corporation. Unless expectations are clearly spelt out, it is nearly impossible to achieve success in turning around a floundering corporation. The corporate turnaround expert is able to remain objective and, like a physician, can diagnose the unhealthy practices that are hindering the well-being of the business. In addition, such an expert can prescribe remedies that will bring about the restoration of good health to a sick corporation. The return to healthy conduct of business may require medication, adjustment of diet, a better exercise program, or a major surgery; and the turnaround expert can prescribe the degree of treatment required to achieve a healthy prognosis.

Since the structure of the company requires that the upper management must function in a healthy manner, healing must begin at the executive level. The board of directors may require the primary course of therapy to initiate the correct treatment program. The other branches of operations may recover by way of a trickle down effect, or they may each require a unique treatment plan engineered specifically for their individual ailments. Only an expert will be able to see the big picture clearly enough to determine the proper plan of care to bring about corporate wellness.

The Essence of Servanthood

Jesus never lost sight of His purpose, and because innumerable people were healed; many heard the true Word of God for the first time; and the whole world was changed because of Him. He was tireless in His efforts to ease suffering and to teach, but He did not always do all the work by Himself. Early on, He recruited others to work with Him. He trained them on the job and held many private training sessions with them. The twelve apostles that He had selected were with Him as He ministered, and He prepared them to continue His ministries after He was gone. He knew He only had a short time, so He worked fervently to train and coach them. He created these alliances with the disciples to enable Himself to reach more people, and to also establish the purpose that would continue through them after He left this world. In all cases, the power of God flowed through Him and eventually through the apostles and disciples commissioned to continue the establishment of the New Testament.

Every good Chief Executive Officer (CEO) knows that his tenure will eventually end. Though no CEO has ever been called on to bear the magnitude of responsibility Jesus bore, one of his or her goals should be to establish a foundation on which the future hinges. Many people are counting on the CEO to man the helm and steer the ship regardless of how rough the journey may be at times. Jesus had to only say to the sea "Peace, Be still!" and the waters became calm. However, for any other CEO it takes a lot of effort and stamina to maintain a steady course. There are crosswinds diverting the course from all sides and countless rogue waves causing turbulence and stress from beneath the surface. Though the CEO is the captain of the corporate vessel, he is answerable to many people, including the shareholders, employees, customers, suppliers, and fellow managers. Many a ship has arrived at port full of sick and disease-ravaged victims. The captain has to be skillful enough to manage the ship in such a way that he or she can prevent disease from infecting the vessel. There must be a competent physician onboard, equipped with all the required preventative medications and health maintenance resources to preserve the health of the passengers and crew. A competent CEO will not wait to call the doctor when his company becomes sick. Instead, like a good ship captain, either he will keep a physician on staff, as a part of the management team or as a trusted advisor to make certain that the corporation is functioning in a healthy capacity. In the same way that the captain manages his crew and oversees the operation of his ship, a good CEO will govern his management team appropriately. He will watch the trends, just as a captain watches the waves, and will steer the corporation away from treacherous waters. Since there are so many entities depending on the capacity of the CEO, trust is a vital component. The customers want a corporation that is able to provide the product or service in a timely manner, with consistently reliable results. The employees expect their leader to make every effort to protect their jobs. The shareholders expect to earn appropriate dividends on their investment. Other managers expect respectful cooperation within the management team. No CEO wants to be forced to walk the gangplank, so it is imperative that the purpose of the voyage be clear, the route mapped out thoroughly and the doctor retained for the trip. No ship should ever set sail without knowing its destination and without a reliable compass for the trip. The business industry is a vast ocean of uncertainty and no one except Jesus has ever had the power to utter a three word phrase, "Peace, Be still", and convince a raging sea to become placid.

The value of tasking and training people to be next in line is well-exemplified in a family owned corporation. The head of the business, which is usually the father, trains his first child to do the management work that if the need arises, the child would take over.

The Ayala Group of Companies is a family owned company that lasted for over 170 years. This is so because the pioneer, Alfonso Zobel de Ayala, has trained his children to get on with the work. It has become one of the most promising businesses in the Philippines and Southeast Asia.

The present CEO of the company, Jaime Augusto Zobel de Ayala, was awarded Management Man of the Year 2007 by the Management Association of the Philippines. More than being a good manager, he is also involved in social development. His mother has impacted a great influence on him, in taking up responsibilities for the people within and around their business.

On Being a Servant Leader

The best asset of any CEO is his or her board of directors. Directors are key players who bring the ideas to the table. Their ideas are like the fuel that drives the corporate engine. They should be the first to ask the questions that customers have not thought of yet. The board must be the ones in the loop who understand the direction that the corporation is following, though they must be guided and steered. They are privy to sensitive information, thus must be trustworthy. It is not always possible for a CEO to handpick his or her board the way Jesus selected His apostles. Enough time should be spent getting to know these people. There must be clear communication within the team. Each corporate director must understand his or her role and be willing and able to comply and cooperate within the team.

Jesus spent countless hours teaching His disciples what they needed to know. His work effectively unplugged them from the unfruitful doctrines that had permeated religious teachings, and he plugged them into the true source of power that flows from the Almighty God. He provided compelling parables that created imagery to make His points understood. He answered their questions and provided concise answers, often using analogies that enabled them to visualize the concept He was teaching. He gave them constant reassurance that they were fully competent to carry out the tasks He gave them. He specified the manners in which He expected them to fulfill their responsibilities. He chastised them if they got out of line, not only because He cared for them but also cared that the purpose of His brief stay on Earth would be fulfilled through them. They did not realize it at the time but He was preparing them for His imminent departure, and that He would not always be in their company. Much like a family owned business, where the parents will pass the company on to their children, Jesus was a leader who was building His staff to take over in His stead.

Jesus' teachings and parables clearly demonstrated that He expected the twelve apostles to continue His work subsequent to Him, in the manner that He had taught them. However, like good and loving children, it is hard to accept that the parents will be gone someday, no longer in place to run the family business. The apostles sometimes have had troubles understanding and accepting that He would be leaving so they told Him with utter conviction that they would follow Him anywhere.

These apostles were men who had been called away from their established careers and who left behind their previous lives to follow Christ. Some, such as Simon, whom Jesus called *Peter*, and his brother *Andrew* were fishermen, as were *James* and *John*, brothers who were the sons of Zebedee. *Matthew* (also called Levi) was a tax collector before he was called, a career considered so dubious and dishonorable that tax collectors were not allowed to testify in court because it was assumed that they were all liars. The previous careers of the others disciples were not clearly spelled out, but they were *Phillip* (a close friend of Andrew), *Bartholomew* (also called Nathaniel), *Thomas* (the doubter), *James* (known as James the Just), *Thaddeus* (who was James' son), *Simon* (known as Simon the Zealot), *Judas Iscariot* (the betrayer who turned Jesus over to authorities for thirty pieces of silver). These men traveled and studied with Jesus for almost three years. They were not only witnesses to the miracles He performed but also participants. Jesus is described in the Bible as being the cornerstone of the Church, and these apostles were destined to become the pillars upon which the Christian Church would be developed.

An Amazingly Fresh New Start

Shortly after forty days of temptation in the wilderness, Jesus began to assemble His group or team. The first three books of the New Testament, known as the synoptic Gospels, basically provide the accounts of the beginnings of Jesus' ministry. It certainly seems appropriate that the first of the apostles were fishermen by trade. Jesus had come to the world in human form to draw humanity to the kingdom of God, to provide a link that empowered men and women to take their petitions directly to God, drawing on the power of the Father by way of the Son, and the symbolic implication of recruiting professional fishermen early in His ministry is noteworthy. The Gospels agree that the first four disciples were all fishermen who willingly left their nets and boats to become "fishers of men". Thus, the testament of a new covenant began with Jesus and His disciples traveling from one village to another where Jesus preached the gospel of the kingdom of God; healing all kinds of sickness and disease that plagued the people. His fame spread quickly and as He traveled, preaching in the synagogues and towns, people began to follow. Often, the multitudes were massive and Jesus would instruct the apostles to minister to the people, essentially using their hands to reach all those who sought His help.

Jesus extended His power to His disciples to heal all kinds of diseases and sickness and to cast out demons. He made it clear to them that this power was from God. Even though they were witnesses to the miracles, and even conduits for Jesus, sometimes the disciples themselves were filled with questions and wonderings about how certain feats would be accomplished. They were often astonished and deeply moved by the magnitude of the miraculous works Jesus performed. They frequently expressed doubts and fears over circumstances that seemed out of control. In each instance that His disciples became alarmed or overwrought, Jesus would dispel their fears by exercising control over the situation. Good examples of this include the tossing of the boat in the storm, and feeding the multitudes on the night of His arrest. In every encounter that seemed unmanageable to the apostles, Jesus exercised authority with calm dignity. Through this manner of teaching, the apostles were able to learn that they too could become empowered to do the work of the kingdom by calling on the power and ultimate authority of God.

Many corporations now are gradually including physically impaired workers, aware of their social responsibilities. They are providing opportunities for people who are intellectually able to do the work but are only physically incapacitated. Many of these workers are speech and hearing impaired but can still effectively work in a corporate environment.

Yumi Taniguchi was born deaf but is now working for BASF Japan Ltd. She arranges import and shipment of material for cosmetics. She goes to the office with her hearing dog Sammy. The dog tells her by touching her body when someone visits her. Q. P. Corporation, also in Japan, also employs physically disabled workers.

Corporations, like what Jesus did, can be instrumental in giving new careers and developing the skills of individuals through opening opportunities for employment. Different people, with or without disabilities, have special skills to contribute to the business when given proper opportunity. Jesus did not undermine the capacity of the people he called to serve with him;

rather he gave them more opportunity to exercise their given gifts and talents. As such, corporations can do the same.

Changing Mankind from Sick & Dying to Alive & Thriving

Jesus did not just focus on teaching his disciples. He saw a dying world, suffering from sick religious practices, unproductive doctrines, and undesirable worldly behavior. He came to modify the actions and attitudes of people by introducing them to a new covenant with God that could change the outcome of their lives. He functioned as a great physician, healing every kind of sickness known to humankind and taught His apostles to also follow in his footsteps. He prescribed a continuing plan of care that initiated the renewal of humanity. He recruited and trained the disciples who would continue to execute His plan after He left His fleshly body. He had clarity of vision and a concise mission statement to fulfill God's plan; and no one has ever upheld a higher code of ethics. No one has better understood human nature or has been so imbued with compassion and mercy. Occasionally, His apostles would need extra coaching because they still lacked complete understanding of His mission.

At a time when Jesus was teaching a multitude about divorce, there were those who attempted to bring little children that Jesus would lay His hands on and pray for them. However, the disciples apparently saw this as an intrusion and attempted to restrain the children. Jesus rebuked His disciples and corrected the situation by telling them not to restrain little children from coming to Him, because they make up the kingdom of Heaven. He clarified that little children are innocent and accepting; and people who have the character like children can easily enter the kingdom of God.

At other times there were those who made requests that were addressed with wise admonishments. When a mother asked that her sons be allowed to sit at His right and left hands in His kingdom, Jesus responded by advising her that it was not His choice to make, but rather that He Himself would sit at the right hand of the Father, and His Father would choose the stations of others. He also indicated that those who would put themselves first in this world would find that they were last in the kingdom of Heaven, and that those who put themselves last in this world would enjoy a first position in Heaven. This further reinforced

His position that willingness to perform servitude to brothers and sisters would be significantly rewarded in Heaven.

The willingness to serve others and to serve the good of an organization as a whole is a fundamental factor to achieving success in life. Whether the consideration is serving customers or family members, setting aside one's concerns to fulfill the needs of others actually pays dividends in the long run.

A number of the more successful corporations are aware and are making efforts to implement corporate social responsibilities like lending help to the less fortunate people, engaging in philanthropy, protecting the environment, and rewarding loyal and outstanding clients.

Petron, one of the largest oil players in the Philippines, has an established corporate social responsibility. It has an umbrella program called Project HOPE – Helping Filipinos Overcome Poverty Through Education. It primarily aims to provide a specialized learning program for the underserved children and youth. It also provides assistance to the children's parents. It also helps the build school buildings in remote areas where there are no venues for educational instruction.

Citing Ambuja Cement again, the company was awarded for Environmental Excellence in 2005. The award was given by Asian Institute of Management Center for Corporate Social Responsibility.

Ambuja is aware that its cement plants could cause degradation in the environment. As such, it continuously employs measures that ensure that the plants maintain low-level pollution. Other than that, since 1991, it has included people in the community as active participants in sustainable development. It provided easy modules on water management, agriculture, and health care.

In the promotion of a business endeavor, it is necessary that it will also take responsibility not only for its clients and customers but also for people who are not direct consumers of its services as well. It must extend beyond its walls. Like Jesus, His grace extends even today when He no longer exists as a human person.

41

The case of some Thailand businesses is a little bit different. Beyond adopting the entire village, helping them to build houses and other infrastructure, the companies have given the village capital for engaging in agricultural business.

Bangkok Glass trained the people in its adopted village to make brushes for the industry. Bata, an international footwear manufacturer, became instrumental in establishing footwear cooperatives, giving the people alternative livelihood other than in the agriculture and sex industries.

Key Learning Points:

- o Having a clear vision, mission, and goal will lead the company to prosperity.
- o Having a well-defined purpose will clearly establish what direction you are going.
- o In order to be a good leader, you must learn first how to be a servant.
- o Corporations must give opportunity to their employees to exercise their given gifts and talents.
- o The willingness to serve others and to serve the good of an organization as a whole is a fundamental factor to achieving success in life.

Chapter 4 - Renewing Hope from Bankruptcy

After a downfall, many corporations have managed to get back on their feet again and become more competitive in their respective industries. Many of these happened due to restructuring and revitalizing management. However, still many more of these establishments have incorporated the Biblical principles, which caused them to make proper clean up and accurate turnaround.

Recovering from Downfall

Many corporations who have suffered downfalls have been able to revitalize their business because their corporate officers are willing to put their customers, their shareholders, and their employees first, before the needs of individual members of management. They have done this by accepting pay freezes or even pay cuts in some cases, thereby restoring greater solvency to the cash flow of the business.

Directors of many such corporations who have been revitalized to a state of corporate wellness have brought in turnaround experts who could objectively survey the sick practices that were harming the corporation and created plans of action that generally involved the cooperation of every interested party. Establishing this sense of teamwork gives everyone a chance to make positive contributions, and it is critical that neither the employees nor the shareholders, nor the customers make unabashed demands that would be harmful to the efforts to restore the company and increase profitability. Key players have their own way of extending help. The employees may make concessions by displaying a willingness to work longer hours, seek ways to be more productive or try a combination of methods as defined by the turnaround team. The customers can assist by paying timely for their orders and by ordering more products or services. The shareholders can help by allowing the turnaround team to prescribe remedies and giving those remedies a chance to take effect without making unwarranted demands that their dividends be increased at a time when the company is still struggling. The directors and managers can help by seeking ways to make the company more profitable, more cost effective, and more self-reliant. Most corporations have found that there are no silver bullet approaches that will fix all their problems and restore viability. It truly takes the efforts of a well-united front to effect a transformation. This is where the corporate turnaround expert is able to provide fundamental insights into pulling everyone together for the good of the whole company. For one group or another to insist that their needs be met first at the expense of all others will be detrimental to the attempt to restore the viability of the corporation. A turnaround expert can be a valuable tool to prevent these demands from occurring in the first place, enabling all groups to win. By delegating roles that lead to successful revitalization, the turnaround team can prevent misunderstandings, resentments, and communication breakdowns that may otherwise threaten the success of the endeavor.

Other members of the team might include the corporation's banks, various governmental agencies, creditors, and/or attorneys. However, the degree of their involvement must be carefully considered and monitored. Often, these entities are highly skeptical and self-protective, which can offset their potential to genuinely assist in promoting the healing of a sick corporation. Nevertheless, they must be accounted for, regardless of whether they are invited to work actively with the corporation in its attempt to bring about its own restoration, or they are spectators objectively scrutinizing the problems needed to be taken into account. This is where a turnaround expert can really shine by sorting through all the various entities that have a stake in the outcome. Those who need to be in the loop will be identified; and those who must remain outside of the scope of critical information will be kept at bay.

Banks are often disturbed by any sign of a downturn and can hinder the success of a turnaround by calling in loans or refusing to loan additional funding that may be required to stabilize the financial outlook of the corporation. It is best to tread carefully with bankers who might be unlikely to contribute to the cooperative effort of other members of the turnaround team. Many banks only wish to become involved with businesses that are showing marked profitability and will shy away from a business that is attempting to recover from a downturn. If they feel too much is at stake they frequently will not be helpful and can actually create injury.

Some governmental agencies can be counted on to offer contributions, such as loan guarantees, grants, and/or tax incentives that will assist in the recovery of the business. These options should be considered if it looks as if they will strengthen the company's ability to recover. In the United States, the Small Business Administration is in place to offer assistance to small businesses. Many corporations that are actually quite sizable find that they are eligible for help.

In China, the government provides subsidies to companies that offer "green" energy alternatives by producing products that use less energy or companies that reduce the amount of energy they consume in the conduct of their business. A good example of these subsidies involves the production of water heaters that are mounted on the roofs of homes in China, where they can collect heat by way of solar energy. Such efforts have also caught the attention of venture capitalists that are joining in the effort to find alternative and renewable sources of energy. Other countries have agencies that also seek to reward the efforts of corporate entities that are attempting to conserve and use renewable sources of energy. It is worth looking at these options to see if the corporation is entitled to such subsidies that might have been previously unknown.

Creditors can be a tough factor to deal with unless they can be called upon to aid in the restoration, by extending balances or lowering payments. Often, they are quite willing to make concessions if they are notified early and provided with viable methods to receive the payments owed to them. Most would rather accept smaller payments over a longer period of time than to lose their claim to the funds, if a company must file for bankruptcy. Ignoring them will only make them become defensive and cause them to file suits that will most certainly hinder recovery efforts. If creditors must be placated with smaller payments, getting them to agree to this course of action is beneficial to everyone involved. Creditors may be willing to offer discounts for lump sum payoffs; though these types of payoffs should be carefully weighed against their impact on the creditors involved.

In addition, it may be detrimental to tie up financial resources, trying to make big payoffs in lieu of investing capital into viable streams of new income. The best solution is to allow the turnaround expert to assess the situation. When mending an ailing company, the prescribed plan of care must be followed as carefully as one must follow doctor's orders to regain health and vitality. Calling on the higher understanding of the corporate turnaround expert will empower the corporation to see various options available.

Price Waterhouse Coopers (PwC), a global business-servicing firm with offices in different countries around the world, offers business recovery programs. Their services include financial analysis and reconstruction, human resources, and performance improvement. It is a corporate turnaround team that can help the business in its recovery from bankruptcy.

One of the clients of PwC is East and North Hertfordshire NHS Trust. The firm helped the Trust to regain business from financial crisis in 2005. It helped remove the inefficiencies from the system. Working with the Trust, PwC had shown the scope of the problem and established solutions that can help in the recovery.

The inputs of attorneys are also helpful especially in situations where laws and jurisdiction need interpretation or clarification. Many attorneys are experts in international law and are extremely useful in ensuring that the interest of a corporation is acceptable in a global market and protected in all the countries in which it conducts business.

Sometimes, following the advice of lawyers during a downturn can have a negative impact if they are too quick to suggest ideas like bankruptcy or liquidation. Typically, *attorneys are not trained to interpret the numbers related to the day-to-day operation of a business; instead, they regard the legal implications of how the business is answerable to other entities.* This information is truly vital to the corporation, but allowing an attorney to pressure the company into liquidating assets to appease creditors or shareholders or overeagerly encouraging the corporation to take their woes to court by any form of bankruptcy, can negatively impact the aim for recovery and might be impossible to overcome in the long run. Usually, as long as there are options still available, it is better to try to revitalize the business than to give up on it altogether. *It is like having a doctor who lets his patient die while there are still alternatives that can cure the sickness.* Though it is not a good indication of management, it is sometimes the immediate resort of many corporations. Again, this is where the specialized understanding of the corporate turnaround expert can deter potentially troublesome entities from gaining too much power over the situation.

If these entities are to be members of the turnaround team, none of them must have overwhelming influence to muscle out other team members. If they can offer no positive remedies, they should be set aside until it is possible to put them to productive use. The turnaround team must be able to weigh the interest and impact of all entities related to the corporation, either directly or indirectly. Then they can devise a strategy that can satisfy the needs of all. The successful revitalization of a suffering corporation requires a concerted effort, honesty, and diligence. There is no room for dissention and it must be dealt with forthrightly. Those who will not contribute to leading the company out of trouble and will not follow the lead of those who will, must not be allowed the opportunity to upset the efforts of others.

Union between Business Mergers

Like a wedding, a business merger is essentially the joining of two separate entities to create one new union. It must too be entered into with proper and diligent consideration about the appropriateness of the union. It is bound to be faulty and unfulfilling, if it is entered into too quickly without due consideration of how each entity will be impacted. It may end up like a union of a bride and a groom who barely know each other and suddenly end up wondering how they got themselves into such a bind.

Since business mergers generally impact more than just a couple of people and a few in-laws, it is wise to bring in professional counselors to assess the viability of the merger long before the process gets to the wedding chapel. In many instances, it is also necessary for governmental agencies to grant a blessing on the union. Corporate turnaround experts can offer powerful advice and assistance in the planning and execution in merging two businesses. The knowledge and expertise provided by the corporate turnaround expert empowers the interested parties to explore the proposition with objectivity and awareness of the full impact of the bond.

To become more powerful and stronger in rendering services, companies like Concerto Software and Aspect Software merged. These companies now operate as Aspect Software. The company has offices in America, Europe, Africa, and Asia and commits to be the largest call center vendor.

Both of the companies support a vision of allowing technology in transforming the way companies interact with their customers. Chief Technology Officer Gary Barnett said that their top priority is to make their customers comfortable and to ensure that they receive enhanced products.

After the high court's approval, Hong Kong's Cable and Wireless HKT Ltd. (HKT) merged with Pacific Century CyberWorks Ltd. (PCCW). PCCW, one of the biggest Internet firms in Hong Kong, proposed the merger after it defeated its rival company, Singapore Telecommunications Ltd. from its bid with HKT's parent company. The union is supported by the shareholders of both companies and is still committed in continuously giving value to their shareholders, customers, and employees.

Your Efforts Are Not Futile, Rewards Will Be Reaped

Jesus did not live a life of luxury and wealth. He explained to his apostles and followers that He, himself, had no place to lay His head. His was a life of servitude to others, spent teaching the God's Word, healing the sick and infirmed, and revealing the rewards that would await those who would hear and act on the truth. He did not sugarcoat the situation by making people believe that all their wants will be rewarded. He taught His disciples that they would encounter trouble and suffering. Still, they willingly stayed by His side and learned the valuable lessons He taught. Though they did not fully understand the consequences, they trusted that they would be rewarded in the end. They had clear and undeniable evidence that the power of God was bestowed to His Son. His promise to those who believed, was a crown of glory in the kingdom of heaven. He provided them with ample evidences of His being a God— walking on the water, acts of miraculous healing and allowing them to witness His transfiguration. His disciples believed and were rewarded with enough evidence that they were willing to endure the suffering He had warned them of. They trusted that in the end everything would turn out as He described. They staked their very lives on it, even unto death. For those who learned to trust what they had seen and participated in, dedicating their lives to continue Jesus' ministry was incomparable to a continuation of what Jesus did.

Many commentators of the Bible have stated that it appears that the disciples expected Jesus to call down an army of angels at the time He was brought to trial by the Sanhedrin. However, even if this were what they had actually expected, that scenario would have defeated the purpose of calling people to faith. The gospel teaches that it was necessary for Christ to be crucified to atone for the sins of the world. Even though He had already foretold those events, His disciples did not seem to understand completely the meaning of what He had taught them until after His resurrection. Only after He had risen did they truly comprehend that there were still many more souls that had yet to come. Finally, in retrospect, they understood the teachings of the prophet Isaiah in foretelling the detailed events of the crucifixion several hundred years before it occurred. It was the realization that there were yet many more souls to be saved that drove the apostles to put their own lives on the line in order to preach the gospel. Jesus had given them no room to doubt that this world was merely a wilderness through which they must pass, bound for a greater reward of an eternal life in the kingdom of God.

Worthwhile rewards are seldom a source of instant gratification, and those that are too swiftly received generally are not lasting and reliable. True rewards come from dedicated efforts to strive for the best interest of everyone involved in a situation. For Jesus, this meant all the souls ever created. He dedicated His life

49

to drawing people away from false teaching, misconceptions, and the doctrines of men that led to doom and failure. His apostles continued His work after He left the world.

True rewards come to those who watch diligently and wait patiently; though, this does not mean sitting idle and procrastinating. Instead, much work must be accomplished, the seed must be sown and truth revealed to those who listen and learn. This message was abundantly clear, depicted in the many parables Jesus taught to His disciples and followers. This principle applies to all who seek to be successful. *Rewards are not all found in the midst of working toward a goal; the reward is in the harvest.*

Each Contribution is Weighed in the Balance

Sometimes it is the small contributions that pay big dividends. On the surface, these efforts to contribute to the good of the corporation may not seem worthy of notice, but they must be recognized that they are also essential to the achievement of success in turning a corporation around. Most of the time, these contributions come from employees who are clear on the mission to save a company suffering a downturn. After all, their jobs are at stake, so most will be looking for ways to help in the effort.

They may be small things like printing meeting notes in black ink, instead of color, and in a smaller font to save ink and paper or forgoing long distance phone calls in exchange for communicating via email to save telephone expense. At a glance, these items may seem insignificant, but if the entire organization embraces these cost-cutting measures, the savings can really mount up quickly and appreciably. During a turnaround, it is prudent and wise to instill this sense of value in everyone who has the ability to impact the bottom line. Many of the most creative ideas in the company come from the people who are performing the productive work. Employees are the first and best line of defense against unnecessary spending and when their suggestions are brought to the table, there is a virtual wealth of information that can be integrated into the turnaround process. A turnaround expert naturally seeks the involvement of those who are performing the daily tasks required, to provide the services or produce the goods of the corporation. *The knowledge and experience of the workforce is one of the richest assets of any company;* therefore, however meager a contribution may seem, it should be weighed in the balance and recognized for its value.

Jesus illustrated this concept to His disciple using the story of the widow's offering in the temple. He watched the wealthy put in their offerings out of the abundance of their wealth, but made particular note of the poor widow who had put in two mites, out of her poverty, which was all she had. He wanted His disciples to realize the difference between giving a little out, and giving all out of one's poverty. More often than not, those who have much to give, only give a small percentage of their wealth, while those who do not have much are giving a greater percentage. In spite of this, those who seem to give a great deal are often shown more respect; while proportionally their contributions are actually more meager than those who are taken for granted.

This point is worth considering when attempting to turnaround a corporation. No one who is working toward this goal should be regarded less worthy of respect than anyone else, regardless of position. Each effort, whether small or big, adds up to the sum total, and is therefore, worthy to be esteemed. Recognition and gratitude should be extended to everyone in the organization who works to achieve a fruitful turnaround. Employee morale can make or break an organization, so keeping employees in the loop and asking for their help in rebuilding 'their' company can be a key factor in executing a successful restoration. The merit of this principle cannot be overemphasized.

Rising Up Amidst the Adversity

Building a bright future amid a troublesome period is a challenge that most companies face at one time or another, just as getting sick is a natural human tendency. Amid adversity, Jesus was able to build His church. Amid adversity, in and outside the corporate walls, a business can also exist.

From a biblical perspective, Jesus came to cure a sick world; and His apostles worked very hard to maintain the health of the church as it grew larger and more widespread. During the time of Jesus, there was much adversity. False prophets were misleading the people and many did not believe in the life of Jesus as the messiah. However, amid that societal illness, Jesus persevered and came to establish the predecessor of many Christian churches today.

After Jesus left, He commissioned His disciples to continue the work. As such, churches in different towns were started. Though members wanted to follow all Christ's teachings, there were still ailments that plagued them. Identifying those ailments was necessary; and the letters exchanged between the various churches showed how steadfast Peter, Paul, James, Jude, John, and all the others were to insist that the church had to be healthy. After all, the church is the body of Christ, and cannot permit any sick members to go untreated.

The situations in the early churches are still true today in relation to corporate wellness. This is true whether we are talking about a person with untreated diabetes, a corporation with unscrupulous directors, or a church with members who are promoting false doctrines. Restoring health sometimes requires surgery, such as removal of a diseased gall bladder, dismissing an unproductive worker or demoting an elder in the church. They are all tough steps but when the health of the entire entity is at stake, tough measures must be taken. Again, this is where it helps to rely on an expert for guidance. The Christian Church has faced such problems in its history and will surely see more problems in the future. This is why Jesus and later His apostles were adamant about relying on scriptural teachings.

The story of the Kenyan Asians who supply pharmaceutical products in Britain is an example of a business that endured adversity. They came all the way from Kenya and were raised in extreme poverty. They supported themselves to college and later established their retail pharmacy businesses. Waymade Healthcare, Sigma Pharmaceuticals, Chemidex, Jumbogate and Neccesity supplies are all such rags-to-riches stories.

Vijay and Bikhu Patel, proprietors of Waymade, are already considered among the richest Asians in Britain. Vijay worked while taking his education at the College of Pharmacy in Leicester. His brother Bikhu, who is an architect, joined later. They developed medicines like palliative and relief for post-operative pains. As a form of corporate social responsibility, they have helped fund schools in Kenya and hold regular medical camps in India.

Supported by his family, Bharat Shah came to establish Sigma, a company concentrating in wholesaling. Their family, including his brothers and now his son, run the operations of the company. The principle of involving everyone in the family for succession made them endure for years.

Many other businesses have survived adversity. Can one imagine how businesses and big corporations exist in war-torn countries? Amid difficulty, these corporations continue to operate with the aim to provide people with more job opportunities, and services to society. Jesus too, amid persecution, strongly endured His mission to be of service to people and to give salvation to the severed humanity.

Trials and Tribulations are Inevitable, be Prepared Always

An established, strong, and competitive business is not a guarantee that in the long run it will not face any trials or tribulation. After all, these stumbling blocks along the way will make a business stronger and experienced. The same is true in becoming a Christian.

Christians in the early times suffered persecution amid their mission in leading more people to God and spreading Jesus' message of salvation. Along the way, Christianity has developed divisions that cause non-Christians to be confused and a bit confounded about what the "true church" of Christianity is and how to identify it. However, the divisions did not cause

Christianity to cease its existence; rather it has become a stronger entity that continued to spread the gospel.

In times that a corporation faces trials and seeks the help of a corporate turnaround expert, the expert should not shoulder all the work. Instead, like Jesus did with His followers, where He allowed people to help Him, hence enabling them to prepare in case the same circumstance occurred again, the expert should give the members of the corporation opportunities ,to exercise hands-on processes and opportunities to manage the situation themselves.

Key Learning Points:

- o Incorporating Biblical principles will help you to stand up again and get back on your feet after a downfall.
- o Union between mergers must be entered into with proper and diligent consideration.
- o Rewards are reaped by those persons deserving it.
- o Even small contributions can pay off big dividends.
- o Preparation is always necessary to overcome tribulations.

Chapter 5 — Starting with a Clean Slate

After standing and getting back on your feet during downfall, the next step is to start afresh with a clean slate. *Without recognizing and accepting the problems, the faults can never be repaired.* The dysfunctional practices in the workplace can cause the downturn of a corporation. They would not only affect the person or team but also affect the whole organization.

Never Reject the Truth

One of the chief factors that led the contemporaneous religious leaders to seek the arrest and crucifixion of Jesus Christ was His unabashed honesty, particularly those forthright observations of the formers' hypocrisy. Though He knew that those set of doctrines had been dictated by the scribes, the Pharisees and the Sadducees were counterproductive to teaching people the true Word of God. Much time and energy was devoted to following man-made rituals and superfluous practices that diverted attention away from the true significance of the Mosaic Law. This nullified the value of the intended lesson by the provision of inspired scripture. Those who were in a position of religious authority imposed rigid expectations on the people, yet they did not conduct their own lives in a manner that reflected the moral standards they professed and upheld. This infuriated Jesus and He frequently chided them, openly and publicly. He referred to them as vipers and hypocrites, rebuked them for stealing the homes of widows, and accused them of shutting up the kingdom of heaven to themselves and everyone over whom they wielded their influence. Clearly, He was describing them perfectly, which made Him a threat to them. For the first time since Moses had led the Israelites out of Egypt, the religious leaders were being held to question and accountable for the disservice they had exacted upon the masses.

Jesus had every reason to be at odds with those religious leaders. The Mosaic scriptures had been provided as a means to guide and encourage humankind to faithfulness to God.

The Ten Commandments had been provided through Moses as scriptural law where adherence to it would ensure God's blessings. However, in the interim of waiting for Moses to return from his journey to Mount Sinai the people had grown impatient and had demanded that Aaron, Moses' brother, fashion them an idol to worship. They gathered all their golden vessels and jewelry, and Aaron created a golden calf. When Moses returned with the tablets where God had scribed His laws, the people were worshipping the idol. Moses was livid. That idol worship was a clear and blatant violation of God's law. Even before receiving the Ten Commandments, people had known that idol worship was wrong and had never participated in such practice while they were in Egypt, but now they did. Thus, it was necessary to establish judges and later kings to rule over the people of Israel to make sure they remained in compliance with God's laws.

Over time, the priesthood had become polluted with many self-focused individuals who cared only to promote themselves as being better than everyone else. They gave very little and demanded much from the people whom they professed to serve. They lived gluttonous and wicked lives themselves; yet they usually passed harsh judgments against the members of their congregations. This was much of what had made Jesus so angry. Hundreds of years before his birth, the prophet Jeremiah had already described the false shepherds, but the religious leaders still did not conform to the principles of God's law. They had either chosen to ignore the message or refused to accept that it applied to them as well. The chief priests and scribes had become like a rampant disease in the heart of Judaism. As a result, the entire body was infused with disease. It was necessary for The Great Physician to come and diagnose the ailment and prescribe the cure. Rather than accepting the diagnosis and treatment, they sought to kill Him. The prophet Isaiah made it very clear that the Messiah would not be accepted and would be surrounded by dogs all around. It was the scribes and Pharisees that stood at the base of the cross and cajoled Christ to call down angels to rescue him from their judgment. One would think that these learned men would have been able to recognize all the clues that were provided to them, but their own self-preservation as men of prominent social status was more compelling to them than the truth. Jesus had described the lawless ones who, though they had a form of godliness, denied the power from which it came. To this day there are many who acknowledge Scripture with lip serve, but live in a manner that disconnects them from the ultimate source of power. Jesus stepped up as the intercessor and was rejected by the ones who should have been the first to recognize Him.

Be Cautious, Nothing is Hidden

An Old Russian proverb states that a fish rots from the head down. In the Biblical times, many religious leaders led people astray instead of showing them the right way. Jesus described this as the blind leading the blind. Likewise, in the business world, *an organization with a corrupt head will surely fail.*

There have been numerous examples of corporations that were wracked with disease at the top of the organization. As previously mentioned, Enron Corporation was headed by a group of unscrupulous leaders. Many members in their management team were actively involved in blatant corruption at the highest level. Accusations of reporting inflated values, fraudulent assets and fictitious profits transpired against members of upper management within the company. Many of them have been convicted of criminal activity with long prison sentences and others, still involved in the trial process. Many charges of insider trading have been filed against those involved in the management of the company. Indictments were handed down on charges such as bank fraud, wire fraud, securities fraud, conspiracy, money laundering and making false statements to auditors and bank officials. These indictments were leveled against those at the highest level of the corporation and many other high-level managers have pled guilty to a litany of other charges.

The corporation had been hailed as "America's Most Innovative Company" by Fortune Magazine for six years running prior to the exposure of the corruption. It has been discovered that upper level management knew for approximately a year that the empire was on the verge of collapse. Rather than taking action to build the corporation into a viable entity, the directors have been accused and convicted of criminal activity that was apparently intended to line their pockets and leave everyone else in the clutch. In addition to bringing about the demise of Enron, other major corporations associated with Enron were also accused of operating corruptly. Most notably, the firm of Arthur Anderson, LLP was convicted on charges of obstruction of justice for shredding documents pertaining to Enron's financial situation. That conviction has since been overturned, but it is doubtful that the firm will ever be restored to its former level of maintaining a highly honorable reputation. They are also involved in other notable corporate corruption cases such as WorldCom, which will also be discussed in this text. For Enron, bankruptcy proceedings followed the fall of this massive corporate empire. Now, the company is merely a shell corporation with no assets and in final stages of dissolution. The employees and shareholders who were not involved in the scandalous practices struggled and many may never recover entirely their losses. Sectors of the corporation like the Prisma Energy International have been liquidated and sold off. Ashmore Energy bought Prisma in September of 2006. Additionally, the original parent company of Enron, Northern Natural Gas Company, has been sold to a group of Omaha investors and has become a unit of Mid-American Energy Holdings Corporation.

The full impact of the scandal that rocked Enron has not been realized yet. There are also political implications in both the United States and the United Kingdom related to large sums of money given by Enron to high-level political figures. Employees and investors lost their savings, children's college funds, and pension funds. The fate of the pension fund is still not fully resolved, though the court has ordered one of the former corporate officials to restore the fund out of his pocket. The shareholders who lost massive amounts of money have yet to be compensated for their losses, though a lawsuit has been filed against the executives who were in a fiduciary position. This situation has become one of the largest cases of corporate dishonor and blatant piracy that the world has ever witnessed.

However, the Enron bankruptcy case has been dwarfed by the magnitude of the bankruptcy case of WorldCom. This was yet another case where some top corporate officials chose to involve themselves in false reporting of financial conditions; and many have been convicted for their involvements. It was actually an internal audit of the books that revealed the false reporting figures. The board of directors was notified and acted quickly to uncover the wrongdoing. The company's assets had allegedly been seriously over inflated by the Chief Financial Officer, the controller and the director of finance. The massive degree of the eleven billion dollar accounting scandal was eventually realized by the end of 2003. However, the company filed a Chapter 11 bankruptcy in an attempt to reorganize. This was the largest bankruptcy ever filed in United States history and the company reorganized merging with Microwave Communications Incorporated (MCI). They moved their headquarters from Mississippi to Virginia and in December of 2005, MCI merged with Verizon after satisfying the U.S. regulatory requirements. However, due to the sheer magnitude of the debt to cash ratio, many affiliated with this case have not been compensated to date, including the fifty-one hundred employees who lost their jobs and did not receive their severance packages due to the filing of bankruptcy. This group has filed a class action lawsuit and the case is pending as of this writing.

These are only two examples of how corruption at the highest levels of corporate prominence has adversely affected the lives of thousands of individuals. The repercussions of such blatant acts of criminal activity resonate far beyond the boardroom and results in the devastation of the quality of life for everyone who is trapped in the trickle down effect. These kinds of cases draw huge media attention but the innocent victims who are deeply wounded rarely receive much media coverage. Even worse, they generally cannot recover what they have lost and any restitution they may receive generally takes years to come. The perpetrators of corporate crime are often portrayed simply as greedy individuals who attempted to take more than they deserved, but there is more to it than that. The kind of person who is willing to participate in such activity may be in it for the thrill of the misadventure, perhaps for the sense of power or maybe for the effect of appearing to have more than they really possess. Regardless of the motivation, there is an underlying lack of concern for how their actions will impact the lives of others; this is also much of what was so unsavory about the behavior of the religious leaders who were called out into the open by Jesus.

The most recent incidents in America have been an eye opener for the whole world. The crash of the Wall street brought down many institutions which were household names and caused a global panic. The greedy perished as the economy cracked up under the pressure and overnight millions of people were facing a bleak future. Lehman Brothers ,Fannie Mae and Freddie Mac, all the giants of American investments, suddenly came into the picture for their greed and for letting the investors down.

Greed has got Americans into this mess. The investors have dumped the asset class finally. The situation was caused by the greed of the private sector institutions and the irresponsible borrowers. Low interest rates and badly formed and executed regulations allowed them the leverage to manipulate the balance sheets way out of proportion, resulting in undue hardships for the common man..

With the car manufacturing industry giants Chrysler LLC, Ford Motor Co. and General Motors Corp in shambles and facing shutdown, it would have a crippling effect on American population and would leave 3 million people jobless and deprive the government of more than $150 billion in tax revenue.

Barack Obama as the new US president has his hands full with so many problems that have besieged America and needs to take stringent measures to bring the economy back to its feet. He has many positive qualities going for him though: he is a man who is from very humble roots and so can see past the veneer of pomp and show. Obama is a man who is driven to go back to the grass roots and sift the poisonous weeds out of the American society, with a group of well educated ministers and competent staff. Is he the New Turnaround Expert of America? The man who will clear the American peoples lives free of falsehood and revive their past glory? Only time will tell.

The American Odyssey

The greed of the Wall Street
Brought the economy down,
Down ,down and out it fell,
Crashing to the ground,
Like a castle made

60

From a pack of cards.

Fuelled by
The greed of the lenders,
Who gave out 'golden deals'
The greed of the borrowers
To 'own' and 'invest'
Homes for homebuyers
Who lived beyond their dreams.

Dreams were provided wings,
Truth and reality forsaken,
The bubble grew....and grew,
And eventually burst
..... shattering all dreams!!

Investors... a shattered economy
Dreams shown by Fannie Mae
Freddie Mac and Lehman,
All too suddenly.. became nightmares
Boomeranged and disappeared
Into oblivion.
Leaving behind...just destruction
A limping , shattered economy.

Was Wall street a villain or
Was it Inherently Stupid
Greedy and Capitalistic?
Whatever it was,
It brought the World
To a great standstill!!
Why do we forget
The simplest lessons are
Always the hardest to learn:
All that glitters the most,
Does not have to be gold.
What sounds too good to be true,
May not be true at all.

Then came Obama,
A new kind of American,
Ready for the problems,
With his feet firmly on the ground!
He promised to clean his feet,

61

To toil and sweep away the dirt,
And work hard to bring back,
Glory to America,
Once again!

Jesus pointed out that they liked to be respectfully greeted in public, they desired the best seats in the synagogue, they desired to have their robes meticulously adorned with embellishments yet, these were the very same people who demanded atrocious tithes from the poor, even to the point of taking possession of the homes of widows if the temple didn't receive enough money from them.

It hurts everyone when those in positions of power and influence are abusive of their power. While the church was supposed to assist widows and orphans, the leaders were using their power to turn them out into the streets, penniless and forsaken. This was why Jesus was so adamant that they had to be exposed for the values they had trampled. Misuse of power will certainly lead to failure and shame. There is no place for it in life, thus no place for it in the corporate boardroom. *It is like building a house of cards and then waiting for the wind to blow, and it surely will blow and the house will fall, leaving victims scattered everywhere.*

Honest Efforts Bring Hope and Revival

A corporation that finds itself in a downward spiral is wise to call in an expert or better still, to establish a team that functions as a turnaround team to assess the causes of the downturn. Chances are there is no corruption, simply minor mismanagement, or miscalculation regarding costs of providing goods or services. *A corporation that is operating honestly has no need to fear the scrutiny of an expert to evaluate their situation.* The desire to build a successful enterprise is incentive enough to initiate the review of practices by a competent expert who can determine where problems exist. Turnaround experts have seen enough of the kinds of issues that cause companies to fail in recognizing immediately the signs of mismanagement. What may not look like a problem to the managers is generally very obvious to the turnaround expert.

For instance, one company had cut its research and development funding by half, from 6% to 3%. It was enough to create a downturn for the entire corporation. Once the expert pointed this out and convinced them to change, there was improvement. Since they were in a highly competitive industry, it was critical to stay on top of the latest developments. To be successful, the business must always assess where the market is headed and researching newer markets, products, and services. It can be compared to continuously taking vitamins to maintain the health of the body. There is a continual need to move forward and stay a step ahead of competitors. Turnaround experts are particularly good at finding the glitches and pointing out the niches that may not be readily apparent to those who are immersed in the daily running of the corporation.

An honest business enterprise that is striving to grow and thrive generally welcomes both positive and negative feedback that will empower them to fix small problems before they become larger and irreversible. Only those companies operating dishonestly need to fear the findings of an outside expert, just as the chief priests and scribes were fearful of Jesus revealing the truth about their actions. God is the truth, and the truth will either find you out or set you free.

There Is No Room for Foolishness

Honesty in business is one of the fundamental keys to success. This is not to imply that everything the managers and directors know should be laid bare on the table for the world to see. That would be irresponsible and totally unnecessary. Honesty simply means that a corporation should strive to earn honest income from honest work as well as honestly treat the shareholders, employees, creditors and competitors. As Jesus said, "Treat others as you want them to treat you". This principle also applies in the corporate world. *If you are engaging in practices that you would not want to be in the receiving end of, do not indulge in the same.* It is simply not worth the risk it brings to the corporation.

Shareholders deserve to be able to invest their money and not have to worry that the directors of a corporation are going to attempt to abscond with the funds, leaving them in the lurch. Employees deserve to be able to go to work each day and not have to worry that an upper level manager will show up and demand that they start shredding documents, or find that their place of employment has been locked up by the Security and Exchange Commission (SEC) or the Federal Bureau of Investigation or any other agency with the power to exercise a cease and desist order. Creditors and vendors expect that the debts owed to them will be repaid in full, without fear that their customer will be filing for bankruptcy because of someone "cooking the books" and running the corporation off into a ditch. *Honesty in business is easier to accomplish than deceptiveness and while the latter may afford a brief spree of mindless wealth, the former will provide restful nights of good sleep.* Honesty is a true friend of wisdom, while deception is a bedfellow of the fool.

The Scripture has a lot to say about fools and none of it is good. In fact, every society throughout the world has famous sayings about fools. Many pearls of wisdom can be gleaned from them, which can easily be applied to business applications.

Scriptural passages about fools tend to remind us that fools do not seem to exert much effort in life. Fools and lazy people are mentioned a lot in the book of Proverbs, none in a good light. However, one of the greatest kings in Scripture, King Solomon, prayed not for wealth or expansion of his kingdom; instead, he prayed for wisdom.

The book of Proverbs states: "The beginning of wisdom is fear of the Lord." There is no room for a corporate executive to act as a fool or attempt to make a fool of others. Wisdom is a fundamental ingredient in building and maintaining a healthy business. Wise decisions lead to success while foolhardiness leads to certain failure. Therefore, it is critical to evaluate the consequences of actions and behaviors that impact the enterprise as a whole. Conscious effort is required to integrate wisdom into business interactions. It is wise to be aware of market trends, technological advancements, consumer demands, actions of direct and indirect competition and potential allies in the business world. A wise CEO watches the world around him or her and attempts to discern how current events will impact the business. In the fast-paced global marketplace, there is a need for constant assessment and adjustment to ensure that the business stays competitive.

Newspapers and magazines are published around the world each day. They present up-to-date information about almost every kind of industry imaginable; thus, a wise company has a constant eye on those reports. Twenty-four hour news reporting is available to further enhance the flow of current information. The internet contains a wealth of vital information and is updated even more frequently than newspapers and magazines. Trade publications are a rich resource for finding upgrades in equipment and techniques that can help a business function more efficiently and more cost effectively. Staying abreast of the ever-changing flow of knowledge is truly a wise move and must be a part of the daily business pursuit for any progressive corporation. *Knowledge, more than power, is economic mobility; and using knowledge wisely is critical to the achievement of success in any endeavor.*

Seeking the Right Answers

Often when traveling, a multitude of people waiting for Jesus' arrival would greet Him and His disciples. News of His impending arrival would reach towns and villages while He was still en route. These massive crowds drew the attention of the local scribes and Pharisees, too, who would then arrive on the scene and attempt to entice Jesus to say something that they could use against Him. However, He had nothing to hide and would answer their questions with unprecedented knowledge and a level of authority that would cause them to be uncomfortable. They were dismayed over the fact that they were unable to trap Him into saying something that was scripturally inaccurate.

Once, when invited to eat with the ruler of the Pharisees on the Sabbath, Jesus was approached by a man suffering from dropsy.

He asked the assembled group of lawyers and Pharisees if it would be lawful to heal on the Sabbath. None answered and Jesus proceeded to heal the man. He went on to ask them if there were any of them who, if they had an ox or a donkey that fell into a pit on the Sabbath, would not rescue the animal. Again, none of them could provide an answer that would contradict the scriptural lawfulness of healing the sick on the Sabbath. It was also the Pharisees who took note of the fact that Jesus and His disciples had not washed according to ceremonial ritual before they sat to eat on another occasion. Jesus was quick to point out to them that while they insisted on following rituals and customs that might clean the outside, their inward parts, particularly their hearts, were filled with filth.

It was also the chief priests who questioned Jesus about whether it was lawful in the eyes of God to pay taxes. He answered by asking whose face appeared on the coin. When they stated it was Caesar's, He told them to pay unto Caesar what is his and to pay unto God what is His.

Attempts to thwart His knowledge were repeatedly met with all the right answers. One can only imagine the anxiety those religious leaders must have experienced when they realized repeatedly that they were faced with a force too powerful for them to even comprehend. The simplicity and compassion with which He taught caused the followers of Jesus to feel compelled to reach out to Him. These were people who were accustomed to suffering punishment and having to offer sacrifice for their sins; then suddenly were in a company of a loving teacher who was instructing them about the loving grace and mercy of their heavenly Father. The dry bones in the valley mentioned by the prophet Ezekiel were being revived by Jesus before the eyes of the religious leaders; yet they were so wrapped up in their own pompous delusions of self-importance that they were oblivious to the truth. However, this was no surprise to Jesus since it was all foreknown.

God had saved the best gift to His children for last, and He knew that the transition to the new covenant would incite the violence that dwelt deep in the hearts of the sons of those who had repeatedly killed His own beloved prophets for many centuries in the past. The uncompromising willingness that Jesus displayed to stand as advocate for the ones who would bruise and crucify Him, and then ask for their forgiveness is truly awe-inspiring.

The Sadducees did not believe in the resurrection and so they attempted to trick Jesus with a question about which brother of seven, a wife would belong to in the afterlife if each brother had died and she had married the next brother, successively until she had finally been married to them all. He answered by stating that after the resurrection there is no giving in marriage. Clearly the question of whose wife she would be becomes moot. They could find no fault with His answer.

The religious leaders tried many times and in many different ways, but were unable to trip Him or cause Him to err in dealing with matters of divine law. At no time, they were able to cause Him to say anything that was inaccurate or opposed to Mosaic Law. Sometimes those who tried to discredit Jesus were simply people who were present within the multitude and clearly upset by His supernatural abilities.

When He cast out demons on one occasion, Jesus was confronted with people who said to each other that He had cast out demons by Beelzebub. This was simply a perfect chance for Jesus to declare that every house divided against it will fail. He was able to convey the fact that the power of God is the only power that can truly exercise dominion over both good and evil. Because God is all-powerful, and Jesus was sent by Him as His intercessor on behalf of humankind, it was clearly the power of God, through Christ, that caused the demons to be cast out. The lessons He taught by way of parables, or by directly stating the matter were all filled with wisdom, concern, and truth. He reached out to people through love and respect for them and they felt it. Most people clearly realized that He was unlike anyone from whom they had ever received scriptural instruction before. His honesty was unprecedented, making Him much beloved and greatly despised at the same time. Those who longed for truth loved Him and those who feared the truth, despised Him.

Golden Harvest

Jesus saw a dying world,
Sick, very sick
Crying for restoration
He was a great healer
Sent unto the earth,

To see, teach and heal,
The hurt of the poor.
With clarity of vision,
He freed from self made prison,
By bringing changes
To the hearts of all.
Ethics were now different,
from ever before.

Followers thronged Him,
Wanting to believe,
Wanting to learn,
Of a better , healthier way.
He taught compassion,
he taught us mercy and care,
He advised to serve others
In adversity to never turn a hair.

True rewards
Are awarded
To those who watch and wait
That too, without any haste.
Rewards are not for working
Towards the goal,
But for staying for the harvest...of Gold.

Jesus Has All the Answers

Of all the Biblical scholars, priests, judges, and prophets who had ever come before, and those Pharisees and Sadducees who were contemporary with Jesus, none could compare with His knowledge of Scripture. He taught with power and authority that had never been witnessed at any time in history. His wisdom was unprecedented. Those who followed Him were clearly struck with a conviction that His power, authority and wisdom came directly from God. His understanding, seemingly by chance, easily convinced even those who simply encountered Him.

Outside of Samaria on a trip to Galilee, Jesus encountered a woman who had come to draw water from the well of Jacob. She was not a woman of Jewish faith, and Samaritans and Jews did not intermingle in society. He asked her for a drink of water, and in return, Jesus offered her living water. Jesus explained that anyone who drinks of the living water, there would spring up within them a fountain of everlasting life. She asked for the water He described. He told her to go get her husband, to which she replied that she had no husband. He then revealed to her that He knew she had no husband and that, in fact, she had already had five husbands and was now with a man to whom she was not married.

The woman was astonished to realize that He knew all about her; and they then discussed that Jesus, Himself , was the long awaited Messiah. Upon the return of His apostles, she went to the city of Samaria and urged the inhabitants to come out to meet Jesus. Many responded and after He taught them with power and authority, such as they had never seen, many were convinced that He was indeed Christ. He stayed in the town for two days, and many other Samaritans became believers. Because of His knowledge of her story, this woman responded by convincing others to take advantage of an opportunity to 'drink of His living water.' An entire village was positively impacted because Jesus was more knowledgeable and powerful than anyone they had ever encountered. His sheer authority was clear and apparent to them and they responded favorably regardless of the fact that He was a Jew. This wonderful example portrays the fact that when the power and authority come directly from God, there are no lines that cannot be crossed. This situation also provided His disciples a preview of the future, since they would later be expected to carry the gospel into the world for a witness, regardless of race, ethnic background, or nationality. Jesus already possessed the knowledge that His ministry would eventually be carried into the rest of the world, so instances such as this event enabled Him to demonstrate to His disciples how they were going to carry on after His departure. Although the political dominion at that time was under Roman rule, there were delineations of religious faith that Jesus knew would have to be broken down in order to establish the new relationship with God that He was setting up during His lifetime. Preparing His disciples for this mission was fundamental and Jesus took full advantage of the opportunity afforded by the visit to Samaria to teach them this valuable lesson.

It had been this same level of power and authority that had astonished so many at the temple in Jerusalem when He had been found there at the tender age of twelve, studying the Scriptures with the elders. He displayed knowledge and understanding that had never been witnessed in one as young as He was. His family had inadvertently left Him in Jerusalem after they had visited the city for Passover. Upon realizing that He was not with them, they went back to find their missing child. When they finally found Him in the temple three days later, they questioned why He made them worry. He responded by stating that they should have known where to find Him and that they should have realized He would be about His Father's house. At that time, they did not understand what He meant, but His mother kept it in her heart knowing that it was indeed His destiny to become the manifestation of God's power and will in the world. She had already been told by angels that He would be the hope and salvation of His people.

At the time of His circumcision, a man of great faith named Simeon had professed his realization that Jesus was the glory of His people, Israel. His childhood was spent growing in the spirit of God and learning. It was a time of preparation for the three years of intense work that would lay the groundwork for the new covenant that would offer salvation to all people willing to accept the truth of the gospel.

Tempered Power and Reasonable Authority

Using power to create positive change is grossly underrated these days. Nevertheless, aspiring to this goal is worthy to be put high on one's list of objectives. To use whatever degree of power one may enjoy to provide for the benefit of others will pay off in the form of dividends, which will be harvested over the passing of time. Unfortunately, throughout history, many have used their power to crush those who were less fortunate. Entire nations have been guilty of extortion of profane proportion and this has caused powerful nations to be viewed with disdain by the smaller, less powerful nations. In a similar vein, authority has been questioned and usurped because some people of authority have sometimes violated the rights of the people under them. Sadly, some governments have demonstrated corruption of authority so heinous that they have committed genocide against some of their own citizens. This causes people to regard leaders with distrust and fear. This does not have to be the case.

The old adage, "power corrupts and absolute power corrupts absolutely" does not have to be adhered to in any arena. It is possible to wield power and authority with knowledge and understanding and to effect positive outcomes for everyone involved. Studying the way that Jesus used His power and authority can provide great insight into how it is possible to be both powerful and compassionate at the same time. Looking at the manner in which Jesus applied His authority throughout the New Testament illuminates the fact that actively embracing one's responsibility, tempering it with loving kindness and compassion, must accompany the exercise of authority.

A good example of the benevolent use of power, influence, and authority was the incident where a group of Pharisees and scribes brought a woman accused of adultery before Jesus. They were prepared to stone her to death, which was the custom of that time as cited in the Old Testament Law of Moses. Clearly they hoped to trick Jesus into saying or doing something unlawful or unscriptural. However, as with all the times the religious leaders tried to trap Him. Jesus knelt and began to write on the ground with His finger as if He had not heard them. They persisted in asking Him as He wrote. He had the power to know the sins of each individual; and He certainly had the authority to convict them all of each sin of which they were guilty. However, His power and authority on that instance provided Him the opportunity to influence their perspectives. He stood up and said that whoever was without sin should cast the first stone. Again, He stooped and continued to write on the ground. One can only wonder what He must have written in the sand about each of them. Whatever it was, He gave them a new outlook on their right to sentence this woman to death for her sin, but also a chance to take an introspective look at their own sins. As each person was struck by his or her own conscience, they dropped their stone and walked away. Jesus stood to see that everyone had left but the woman and He asked where her accusers were and if none had condemned her. She said there was no one, and He replied that neither would He convict her.

While Jesus had the authority and power to convict them all of every sin for which they were guilty, He used His immense compassion to cause them to look within their own hearts and realize that none were without sin.

The use of power and authority to do well or to do harm lies within the grasp of every leader. Following the examples of Christ to temper power with compassion, and authority with reason paves a path to success. Drawing comparisons between societies led by benevolent and sensible leaders against societies led by ruthless and reckless leaders strengthens the argument that Jesus provided the right answers. His answers were always the ones that pertained to fairness and provided the means to generate a positive outcome.

Key Learning Points:

- o Without recognizing and accepting the problems, faults can never be repaired.
- o A growing and thriving business generally welcomes both positive and negative feedback that will fix small problems before they become larger and irreversible.
- o Honesty in business is one of the fundamental keys to success.
- o Wisdom is a fundamental ingredient in building and maintaining a healthy business. Wise decisions lead to success while foolhardiness will lead to certain failure. Therefore, it is critical to evaluate the consequences of actions and behaviors that impact the enterprise as a whole.

Chapter 6 — Adherence to Law and Governing Ethically

Jesus has all the answers, and He, himself lived in a society where spiritual, moral, and governmental laws existed. In our present context, we still live in such a society. As such, you and your business are bounded by laws. You should adhere to those laws and govern your business ethically and morally.

What Does It Takes To Be Lawful And Ethical?

Driving the success of a corporation involves more than the hard work in executing the day-to-day operations. *A truly successful business must maintain utmost integrity when it comes to matters of corporate conduct.* The consequences of functioning otherwise have been well demonstrated by the demise of Enron and other corporations that have fallen due to unlawful and unethical behavior of the management team. The concept of ethical and lawful corporate conduct is not a new idea. The tenets of these concepts are well documented in both the Old and New Testament. Laws and statutes pertaining to appropriate corporate conduct are in place to protect and promote the well-being of everyone in a given society. Every industrialized nation has enacted laws and regulations to protect their citizens, promote fair trade, and prevent corruption. Corporate laws provide a level playing field for the business enterprise and prevent opportunity for confusion concerning what is or is not appropriate.

Throughout every society, laws have been the basis of social order. When Moses returned from Mount Sinai with the Ten Commandments the Israelites were better equipped to abide by God's requirements, having them spelled out in specific terms. In addition to the Ten Commandments, provisions were created that established penalties for violating those laws, further creating order in the system. Knowing what is expected and anticipating specific consequences for disobedience is critical to social stability. A lawless society would be dangerous and unproductive. God, Himself, set the precedent for humankind to establish proper rules for governing the populace, all for allowing people to live healthy, productive, and satisfying lives. Jesus was born into a time when the Roman Empire ruled and He encouraged people to abide by the law and adhered to it Himself. Additionally, there were religious laws pertaining to taxes paid to the temple, and again, He submitted to the authority of those laws. Jesus diverged from the common interpretation of Mosaic Law pertaining to the Sabbath. He practiced sensible compassion by healing those who approached Him at the temple on the Sabbath, but this was not a violation of the law. Jesus upset the religious leaders, but successfully demonstrated that showing this loving compassion on the Sabbath actually upheld the Mosaic Law that commanded people to love their neighbors. Jesus successfully changed the hearts of His followers and made them realize that caring for others was not opposed to the law pertaining to honoring the Sabbath.

When individuals or groups make the choice to break the law it creates injury to someone, either directly or indirectly. While it is true that there have been some unreasonable laws created from time to time, in some place or another, as a whole, regulating society through the enactment of laws, statutes, and regulations is a noble aspiration that promotes public well-being. In addition, operating with a great level of integrity will benefit all involved in the long run. A Bible Proverb states, "The one who lives with integrity lives securely, but whoever perverts his ways will be found out."

Clarifying Terms of Agreement

In the global marketplace, now more than ever, it is critical to establish manageable contracts that will spell out how disputes should be resolved among parties who are conducting business in different countries. In an ideal world, there will be fluid transactions where everyone profits, but in the real world, this will not always be possible. Making such a decision in advance protected the financial interest of a Japanese computer company regarding a dispute with a Chinese distributor. Because the two companies had agreed in advance that any disputes that might arise would be handled in court in Hong Kong, the case was easily settled to the benefit of the Japanese company, which might not have been the case had the matter been placed in the hands of a Chinese court. This is how critical it is that such provisions be spelled out at the commencement of business among international entities.

While there are international laws that pertain to the conduct of import and export business, often the host country of one or the other of the entities will attempt to flex its legal muscle to give more credence to the claims of the company from its own jurisdiction. Lawsuits create hurdles that are best avoided. The easiest way to avoid such conflicts is to make sure that well-defined agreements exist and properly executed by the parties involved. In addition, remedies for disputes should also be woven into the fabric of the agreement. While it still may be necessary to have lawyers unravel the details for examination in court, those basic threads of the agreement will provide insight into the intent of the covenant that will influence the final outcome. The money saved by avoiding unnecessary conflicts can better be invested into the growth of the corporation.

Jesus was Himself a covenant, a new covenant between God and all of humankind. He left His throne in heaven to proclaim and clarify God's purpose and intent for humans, and to provide a means by which everyone could establish a meaningful relationship with God. The new covenant He provided replaced the sacrifice of the blood of lambs and bulls with the sacrifice of His own blood. His death on the cross caused the veil to tear between the inner temple, known as the Holy of Holies, and the outer temple. This was significant because no one could enter the Holy of Holies except for the high priest and only after their own sins had first been atoned for through a sacrificial animal. Because the death of Christ tore the veil, people could begin to approach God directly with their prayers, as Christ has already become the intercessor. He is now the advocate who is willing to plead the case of everyone who loves Him.

Negligence of the Law Excuses No One

The Bible demonstrates the value of submitting to established laws. It is reflected both in the Old Testament and the New Testament. Jesus was unmistakably clear on His position on submission to lawful authority. First and foremost, He upheld the Ten Commandments as supreme law that must be obeyed above all else. He specifically stated that He had not come to change one jot or title of the law but He came to fulfill them. Later, the Apostle Paul stated that the law is good if a man uses it lawfully.

There were those who did question the lawfulness of Jesus' actions taken with regard to healing people on the Sabbath, but He was able to aptly set aside those questions by providing analogies that made it clear that He was not violating any of the law.

When Jesus healed a man on a Sabbath, many people condemned him because it was unlawful to work on that day. However, Jesus with full conviction showed them that he was not violating any law but showing compassion to people on a holy day. He did not equate the extension of compassion as being a form of work. Instances like that provided people proper perspective in interpreting the law. That is why it is important to spell out clearly the expectations of the law and how they apply in a given situation. God had accomplished this with the Ten Commandments, but men had misconstrued the purpose and intent, making it necessary for Jesus to provide clarification regarding the difference between doing work and exercising common sense. It could further be noted that those religious leaders disregarding the suffering people. This was a direct violation of God's commandment that people should love their neighbor. Scripture does bear out the fact that Jesus held the particular commandment to love one another in highest regard, second to loving and honoring God. He further asserted that it was imperative that we love everyone, not just those who are our friends and family. He encouraged us to pray for our enemies, to turn the other cheek when we have suffered a wrong, and to give up our tunic and our cloak when we have been sued for only the cloak. Doing what is right, and going above and beyond what was previously expected, instills knowledge of righteousness for which rewards will follow.

Bitter embattlements are a waste of time and energy, leaving everyone involved with resentments and disillusionment. Following the principles set forth in the lessons that Jesus taught increases the desire to resolve conflict rather than to remain

76

embroiled in hostility. Creating resolution among disparaged entities may open an opportunity for them to resume amicable relations at a later time. By teaching people to mend relations rather than to sever them, Jesus reinforced the importance of God's commandment concerning loving one's neighbor as oneself.

On another note, however, Jesus made it clear that if something is intrinsically wrong, it must be eliminated. He used exaggerated metaphors to emphasize the importance of restraining oneself from participating in sinful behavior. He instructed that if your eye causes you to sin, pluck it out and cut off your hand that does you evil. Though He did not expect His followers to truly disfigure themselves physically, He made them realize the significance of keeping away from all forms of behavior that may hold them in the bondage of sin.

To participate in wrongdoing in any form is sure to lead to doom and failure. Any short-term gains that might be realized through illicit activities will be offset in the long run, and the penalties will be severe. Some illegal and immoral practices might not seem to be criminal, but the impact they carry will affect many people through a ripple effect. This is why it is important to always maintain integrity in the conduct of ones business dealings. Devious dealings create enormous amounts of stress and are hard to conceal. The amount of work involved in covering lies and deception can be overwhelming; and when considered in proportion to using that same energy to work toward an honest goal, it takes a lot more work to be dishonest than to be honest. Even the slightest hint of dishonesty should be 'cut off' immediately before it becomes an abyss ,capable of swallowing the entire corporation and everyone in its wake.

Illegal Insider Trading Brings Forth Destructiveness

A modern day example of using ones eyes and hands to do evil is participating in illegal insider trading. It is defined as a breach of fiduciary duty by buying or selling stock while in possession of material non-public information about the state of a security. While it has been mentioned earlier in relation to Enron, this topic deserves a more detailed examination. *One of the most crucial considerations when dealing with a publicly held corporation is avoiding any appearance of impropriety.* Illegal insider trading has been in the spotlight in recent years in the United States as the SEC has brought legal action against corporate officers and shareholders who have violated the law concerning stock trades. Many such cases have resulted in dramatic court trials that have attracted extensive media coverage, including the Enron case discussed earlier. This kind of media coverage can annihilate the viability of a corporation, even if it is later found that there was no wrongdoing. Healthy trading of stock in a publicly held corporation infuses capital into the company that strengthens its overall economic standing.

While prices may rise and fall within reasonable parameters on a daily basis, major changes involving mergers or acquisitions, new product announcements, workforce downsizing and changes in lending rates can have greater impact on stock prices and trades. Those in positions with insider knowledge concerning such fiduciary elements are obligated to refrain from taking advantage of this confidential knowledge by purchasing or selling securities these types of situations can impact.

While it is not illegal for corporate officers, directors and employees to trade stock they hold in their own company, it must be done within specific guidelines dictated and overseen by the Securities and Exchange Commission. Specific guidelines are in place to protect the interest of all shareholders. Those who are in the position of having proprietary fiduciary knowledge about the corporation should adhere to those guidelines.

Generally, those participating in illegal insider trading may do so to earn higher gains than they would if the information had first gone public as is required, or to avoid losses that will be incurred upon public notification about a decline in the status of the security. These activities can involve corporate directors, officers, or employees who have traded stock based on any non-public material knowledge about a security.

Outsiders can also become involved in insider trading by way of "tipping" which can leave them subject to severe fines, penalties and even imprisonment if they are found guilty in a court of law. Tipping cases can involve such individuals as family members, friends, vendors, bank officials, government officials or anyone else who is privy to confidential inside information and uses it as a basis to buy or sell stock. The SEC is watchful of any kind of trading that undermines the fair exchange of stock among shareholders. Their goal is to uphold the integrity of the securities exchange process by insuring that trades are transacted in a fair and equitable manner.

Currently, most major corporations have programs that explain what is acceptable and what is not, when it comes to trading stock, what behaviors are considered inappropriate or illegal, and how to legally buy or sell stock in the company. There are generally blackout periods during financial reporting timeframes that prohibit officers and employees from entering into transactions that could be considered illegal or unethical. The purpose of providing educational information to officers and employees is to prevent anyone from inadvertently becoming involved in a situation where even the appearance of illegal activity can be argued. *It is critical to take material fiduciary information very seriously and to never reveal confidential information about the financial status of a corporation that is not publicly available.* If a merger is in the works, a new product or service about to be launched, or an adverse condition exists that will affect the value of shares, there should be no trading until such time as the information has been made public for a specified period of time. Taking advantage of educational material pertaining to legally trading corporate shares of stock is a sound business decision that will enhance the strength of any corporation. Corporate turnaround experts are a valuable resource for obtaining advice and expertise in this area. They have seen the consequences of negligence with regard to keeping a watchful eye on how critical information has been handled. They can provide badly needed insights to help keep your company from being involved in or accused of inappropriate activities.

Jesus clarified the difference between enjoying abundance in one's life, accumulated by virtue of one's labors and accumulating wealth and treasures through covetousness. He instilled to His followers the belief that their labors for God would be rewarded with blessings while showing that those who covet wealth will receive no blessings beyond their possessions. In the synoptic Gospels, Jesus warned against laying up treasures on earth to be corrupted by moth and flame or stolen by thieves. He indicated instead that it is better to lay up treasure in heaven by living a life that is pleasing to God.

Millions of Christians forgo illicit ventures that could yield them enormous sums of money, simply because they involve wrongdoing. People practicing biblical principles are not willing to perform such transgressions under the watchful eyes of God. Because Jesus addressed every conceivable social issue, even taxation was cited in His message.

The Necessity of Taxation to Social Order

Another factor that pertains to the effective operation of a corporation revolves around taxation. Corporations enjoy the benefit of tax breaks that allow them to maintain a higher level of operating capital. Sometimes, people complain that many businesses have too many tax loopholes and that the burden of taxes falls on individuals. The truth is that corporations do have large expenses that most people do not fully realize, so corporations should be entitled to whatever tax breaks are available to them.

Many individuals have no concept of the costs associated with paying for unavoidable items like insurance, worker's compensation benefits, and matching tax amounts withheld from employee payroll. Many large corporations pay a huge portion of the major medical benefit expense for their workers and contribute to pension funds directly from corporate earnings. These elements all add up to big expenses that are paid directly from the gross earnings of the corporation. Certainly, a wisely managed corporation should attempt to avoid overpaying taxes though it is equally as important to report earnings honestly and pay the correct amount of taxes as required to operate lawfully. Willfully hiding earnings to avoid taxation is one of the surest ways to set up the demise of the corporation.

80

While average people might bemoan the legal tax breaks that large corporations have at their disposal, those same people will become seriously outraged if they learn that a company has illegally manipulated the system. A sure way to alienate potential customers and destroy the future of a company is to be accused of tax evasion. Even worse, to be found guilty of evading taxes is costly in the long run. Fines and penalties might ravage any short-term gain.

Taxation is not a new concept; it is as old as humankind is. Every society has been subjected to some form of taxation and there have been some civilizations that suffered such cruel standards of taxation that multitudes of people were thrown into debtors' prisons or forced into lives of servitude, all for the sake of taxation.

It was no different in the time Jesus walked the earth. He was tested by the Pharisees who sent their disciples to inquire of Him whether it was biblically lawful to pay taxes to the Roman government. To reiterate the response indicated in a previous chapter, Jesus had them bring Him a denarius and asked them whose image and inscription was engraved upon it, to which they replied that it was Caesar's. He told them to render unto Caesar what was Caesar's and to render unto God what is God's. Though their goal had been to trip him on a religious legality, they were astonished that His answer could not be contested.

On a different occasion, when Jesus and his apostles had arrived in Capernaum, the temple tax was requested of Jesus through Peter. When Peter approached Jesus about the temple tax, Jesus sent him to the sea to catch a fish with a hook. Peter was told to take the first fish that came up and look inside its mouth, where he would find a piece of money to pay the temple tax. *Jesus expressed no objections to paying taxes.* He encouraged His followers to be law-abiding citizens. Likewise, *He taught the same to His apostles who continued to teach the virtue of paying one's rightful dues.*

Key Learning Points:

- o Laws bound you and your business. You should adhere to those laws and govern your business ethically and morally.
- o A truly successful business must maintain utmost integrity when it comes to matters of corporate conduct.
- o Knowing what is expected and anticipating specific consequences for disobedience is critical to social stability. A lawless society would be dangerous and unproductive.
- o God, Himself, set the precedent for humankind to establish proper rules for governing the populace, all for allowing people to live healthy, productive, and satisfying lives.
- o Jesus made it clear that if something is intrinsically wrong, it must be eliminated. He used exaggerated metaphors to emphasize the importance of restraining oneself from participating in sinful behavior.
- o Even the slightest hint of dishonesty should be 'cut off' immediately before it becomes an abyss capable of swallowing the entire corporation and everyone in its wake.
- o Willfully hiding earnings to avoid taxation is one of the surest ways to set up the demise of the corporation.

Chapter 7 — Having the Right Master-Servant Relationship

Jesus was clear on His ways to relate to His followers. He also exemplified the relationship between a master and a servant in many parables. Businesses as such, also operate with a management on top and many employees as subordinates. In this case, businesses can adopt many of those teachings in their operations.

A Worthy Servant and a Fair Master

Jesus, and later His apostles, taught valuable lessons concerning the relationships that ought to exist between a master and hired help. His apostles and the seventy Good Samaritans that were sent out ahead of Jesus as He traveled from town to town experienced many lessons about earning one's own way. They were instructed to take nothing with them, but to enter a home and stay there, accepting the generosity of the host as their compensation. This enabled them to travel freely, not hindered with provisions. As such, they were able to spread the Good News quickly and efficiently.

On another note, however, Jesus admonished all servants to be watchful that they provide diligent service to their master, regardless of whether or not they knew precisely when he would be returning. To do otherwise would leave them open to recrimination. Those who did not know, but demonstrated poor judgment would receive lesser punishment than the servant who knew exactly what was expected and still failed to be prepared. *He made it clear that anyone who receives much, much is expected in return; and, the more one receives, more is also expected.*

These lessons apply to those for whom God has provided, but they aptly apply to individuals in the workforce, as well. No employer wants to be concerned that if they are away on business, their employees are shirking their responsibilities. It is wrong for employees to take advantage of their employer; anyone hired must be worthy of their pay. The entire Bible is rich with information about how God perceives those who work in contrast to those who are lazy. On the other hand, Scripture also teaches that employers are not to take unfair advantage of their employees. Fair pay is expected to be provided in exchange for the efforts of workers. Jesus set an example Himself while teaching and managing the disciples He had chosen. He treated those men with respectful consideration, offering instruction and guidance through every endeavor they undertook. He made sure their needs were continually being met and even offered His own servitude to them, such as had not been demonstrated by an authority figure before. Though, He was their master and teacher, Jesus unreservedly washed the feet of His apostles to demonstrate service to each other. The work He performed throughout His teaching period were done for the Glory of the One who sent Him. His unequivocal dedication to God was apparent in His kindness, healing, and teaching. He professed that the Father provided His power to do all things. He thanked to God in all things and set an example in giving due reverence and respect to the Creator, to for all those who believed in Him.

Jesus did not ask of His disciples anything that He was unwilling to do, and in fact, worked much harder than He asked for them to work.

Faithfulness in the Least, Gain Much

Jesus provided numerous examples of the relationship structure that was implicit between a master and servant in His parables. He related stories about good and bad masters and servants. Each parable demonstrated specific behaviors and consequences to their actions.

Jesus stated in a parable that to be faithful with much, it is necessary to be faithful with the least. *One who is not trustworthy with a little responsibility cannot be counted on to live up to a big responsibility.* As such, employees should stay faithful even at the least of their responsibilities.

On Enhancing Employee Relations

Most employees will not be called upon to put their very lives on the line for their job. Other than soldiers in the military, most people never have to encounter much physical risk in relation to their work. Dedication and loyalty are the least any employer should be able to expect from their workforce. Many passages of Scripture speak of the employer-employee relationship and offer solid advice that can be applied in the workplace.

Jesus illustrated this kind of relationship numerous times in parables; in each instance, He promoted fairness on both sides. Christian business leaders enjoy successful relationships with employees because they study and apply the teachings provided in the Bible. Likewise, Christian employees respect their employers and apply the teachings in their desire to show respect to God by upholding their worldly responsibility to their employer.

A good employee will look for ways to advance the best interest of the company and will provide productiveness from the time their day commences until the close of business for the day. Respect for authority and allegiance to the corporation are vital characteristics of a good worker. Workers who offer less, are hindrance to the welfare of the corporation and must be dealt with strongly, to avoid the destructive effects they can create. At times, it may be necessary to discipline employees who are not living up to their obligations. This may come in the form of a verbal reproach, a written reprimand, or dismissal from employment. Most employers offer a step by step process for dealing with disciplinary issues among their workforce and attempt to give their employees every opportunity to step up to the task before relieving them of their job. It is always in the best interest of the company to try to assist employees in achieving the desired level of competency. Replacing a worker is usually more difficult and costly than reforming one, but if it becomes apparent that the employee will not readily adapt to reform, firing them may be the only option left.

Christian employers who attempt to use biblical principles to relate to their workforce sometimes struggle with such an unsavory issue, but *as long as every effort has been made to rectify the situation, there is nothing wrong with letting someone go if they don't work as required.* Quite the contrary, an unproductive employee can negatively impact the entire organization by upsetting the morale of their peers, wasting the precious resources of the company, and damaging the esteem of their managers. Such conditions simply cannot be allowed to exist and it may be necessary to weigh the good of the whole against the good of the individual.

Naturally, good business sense will dictate that the organization comes first. Besides, it really does not help anyone to let them get by with doing less than their best. People who are not working up to their potential may be unhappy in their position and setting them free affords them the chance to look for whatever it is that makes them happy.

This is not to imply that everyone is going to perform at one hundred percent every day, but all in all, every employee is expected to perform at a specific level on average. There should be consistency of performance that can be measured. It is helpful to have responsibilities specifically spelled out by way of job descriptions for every position in the company. A detailed job description is an effective tool that can provide employees with clarity of purpose, and managers with the documentation they need to assess how well each employee is performing. Knowledge of what is expected of them empowers the workforce to strive for specific benchmarks. Thus, it is easier to collect feedback because there are particular items that can be measured based on the job description. Occasional evaluations, provided in a timely manner, will assure the employee that they are meeting their potential or advise them if they are off track.

Knowing the status of their performance helps them be a better employee by affording them the badly needed insight into what is working and what needs improvement. Fair and equitable assessments strengthen the backbone of the company and must be considered as one of the most valuable tools for maintaining the smooth conduct of business. A corporate turnaround expert can offer indispensable information concerning how to set up job descriptions and standards for evaluating workers. Objectivity is needed to insure that appropriate criteria is established for measuring productivity and to make sure that subtle aspects of an employee's responsibilities are not overlooked in the process of creating their job description. Sometimes it is the subtle differences in responsibilities that set one worker apart from another. This is often a result of their specialized training or specific education, which should be considered when their performance is being assessed. Determining the significance of these distinctions is a typical proficiency of the experienced corporate turnaround expert. Corporations who have taken advantage of the talent provided by experts in this arena have found that they have been able to enhance the quality and quantity of work being produced. They have also learned that their employees are happier and more eager to promote the best interest of the company if they have the means for gauging their level of contribution to the organization.

Another effect of measuring and assessing proficiency of the workforce is that it makes it easier to ascertain whether wage rates are appropriate for those who are creating the products and providing the services to the customers. Classification of jobs and standards for compensating workers helps corporations maintain a set of pay scales that pertain to each position within the company. Many factors such as demographics, educational requirements, industry standards, job responsibilities, and many other dynamics will affect the numbers reflected in those pay scales. A turnaround expert is a vital resource in evaluating the practicality of the compensation program that the corporation is using. It may be necessary to make adjustments to an existing program to help the corporation become more competitive with its peers. The need to make such adjustments is best deferred to the judgment of an expert to avoid making stabs in the dark of this issue. If the pay scales of a corporation are too far out of line with industry standards, it can have a severely damaging impact on the bottom line, regardless of whether the scales are set too high or too low.

If the pay scales are set too high, it may signal the need to freeze wage increases for a time or take other measures that bring wages in line with industry standards. It is like putting the cart before the horse to attempt to bring wages down. If they are already set too high, the corporation risks loss of good workers, distrust, and humiliation and adjustments may not be worth considering. However, if excessively high wages in proportion to earnings is linked to corporate downturn, action must be taken.

Most employees are respectful of honesty and the earnest quest of their employer to recover from a downturn. Sometimes if pay cuts are required, the employees will accept them willingly rather than to risk losing their job entirely if the company is forced to go under. This, of course, is a worst-case scenario and one that revolves around the concept that the cause is, in part, related to excessively high wages. However, if this scenario describes the reality of the situation, reliance on a corporate turnaround expert to help the corporation navigate this minefield is substantially safer than trying to go it alone. The corporate turnaround expert is willing to absorb the scorn and bear the brunt of the disdain that this kind of process is likely to create. This leaves the managers and directors in a better light than if they campaign for such a measure on their own. Such an expert is generally very good at explaining the reasoning and logic that has preceded the necessity to take this type of drastic measure. Corporate turnaround experts are particularly good at rallying the workforce behind measures that, while appearing negative in essence, offer long term rewards that can be enjoyed by those who will contribute to the effort.

After all, if the employees decide not to help restore the company, they are forfeiting their chance to build a future with a corporation that may be standing on the cusp of true greatness. A corporate turnaround expert is able to relate to them in a way that permits them to grasp the big picture and generally can muster the support of the majority of employees. At the other end of the spectrum is the issue of excessively low wages that can deter talented applicants from pursuing employment with your corporation.

The old saying that anything worth having is worth paying for, holds true when it comes to building a great workforce. Great employees are the backbone of any truly successful corporation. It is the wise and prudent manager who takes the time to review pay scales within the company and compare them to similar industries within the region to determine how closely employee wages align demographically with those of other employers.

While it may not be practical or possible to enact substantial wage hikes that can bring a company up to sufficient standards right away, being knowledgeable about appropriate wage structuring provides insight into how the corporation can progressively move towards providing the grade of wages that will attract the best talent. Companies have become more competitive in their offerings to attract well-educated, motivated, and competent people to fill the ranks of the workforce. This is an area where a corporate turnaround expert can provide enlightenment and advice.

One of the most celebrated issues of unjust wages was the case of Nike. Nike is one of the most popular brands of shoes all over the world. However, it was accused of exploiting its workers.

First, the shoes were made in South Korea and Taiwan but since local labor cost became too steep for the company, it transferred the manufacturing to Vietnam and China — countries where minimum wages cannot even feed a family, and where labor unions are prohibited.

Wages to workers formed less than an eighth of Nike's high final selling price. Take for example the cost of labor in making a pair of shoes; it was only $4.90 while it would be sold for around $150.

To counteract all the accusations, Nike issued a huge press release yet it was unable to change the views of people about the company. Those counteractions did get into the root of the problem — not paying its workers a living and just wage.

Catholic Human Resource Executives said that employers and employees are partners in establishing the company. A just wage is part of the employee's benefits intended to safeguard and promote sustainable lives for them. Wages should not only include salaries but also health care, rest periods, opportunities for self-improvement, and protection from injury.

Dealing with Prima Donna Type of Personality

Dealing with personnel issues is complex and touchy; however, managers who take the initiative to confront this subject head-on are more likely to achieve the positive results they desire. Managers must work closely with their teams and with individuals under their supervision. However, it must be recognized that each person should possess a set of skills that serve as a tangible asset and each team must function as effectively as a machine. While some individuals will require a higher level of supervision, others will be able to function at a level that requires very little regulation, and this generally creates a balance that works well.

An interesting phenomenon that has taken place over the past couple of decades is the demise of the Prima Donna type employee. This kind of person is typically very aggressive and demanding of others, often demeaning and demoralizing the people who work closely with them. While they may generate numerous sales leads or a high volume of sales for the company, it is often at the expense of others with whom they work. There were times that these kinds of people were allowed to run roughshod over their co-workers because they were regarded as high performers, but this has become an unacceptable behavior in today's corporate world. These days, teamwork is considered very critical to the success of the company and those individuals who once enjoyed star status are finding themselves outside the acceptable scope of behavior. Close observation over time has proven that building a cooperative team, with each member being treated as an integral part of the whole is more conducive to success than to allow a single individual to take an inordinate amount of credit upon him. While it is very desirable that some people on a team be driven, aggressive, and first-rate performers in their class, these people cannot be allowed to enjoy celebrity status that causes others to be debased. This is an area where a corporate turnaround expert can be very helpful. Not only can such an expert recognize the signs of this kind of situation, they have all the tools required to address the problem.

A team member who consistently demands the spotlight, who minimizes the contributions of fellow associates, who has fits of anger or just behaves in a haughty manner must be reined in and brought under control. They must understand that they cannot exhibit this kind of behavior in the workplace and expect to remain employed. Their tendency to intimidate and humiliate their co-workers cannot be tolerated and they must be humbled. Often, the mere threat of loss of employment is enough to humble this kind of individual; but sometimes, if they refuse to align with the team, it is necessary to just let them go. While this may seem frightening, particularly if this person appears to be a top performer, if their bad behavior is affecting others in a negative way, there may be no other options. Sometimes employers have been faced with this situation and have learned that their Prima Donna was not even the true source of high performance; it was in fact the team of which they were a part. The spotlight was undeservedly fixed on them. After removing the Prima Donna from the picture, the contributions of others can be recognized and rewarded appropriately. Again, this is where the objectivity of a corporate turnaround expert can be insightful and indispensable.

Looking back to how Jesus dealt with the disciples, one sees that He was clearly fair and provided equitable recognition to them all. When they did try to exalt themselves above their peers, He dealt with them forthrightly and immediately. Even when the mother of two of His disciples asked that her sons be allowed to sit at His right hand and His left hand in heaven, Jesus tactfully told her that she did not realize what she was asking. His own life was dedicated to servitude to those around Him. By His own example, Jesus demonstrated the positive power of remaining true to the cause, as opposed to seeking to exalt oneself.

Many times during Jesus' travels, there were instances where the apostles or those who would be disciples, attempted to promote their own self-interest; but in each situation, Jesus would successfully clarify the futility of being so self-centered. Jesus was actively building a team that would be prepared to carry on His work in the world after His return to Heaven, so He patiently instructed His disciples on the art of working toward the common good. Because He had attended to the needs of those around Him — washing the feet of the disciples, feeding thousands at a time and admonishing them to work for their keep — Jesus was the most exemplary role model the world had ever seen.

Key Learning Points:

- Jesus admonished all servants to be watchful that they provide diligent service to their master, regardless of whether or not they knew precisely when he would be returning.
- Anyone who receives much, much is expected in return from him; and, the more one receives, the more he expects.
- It is wrong for employees to take advantage of their employer; anyone hired must be worthy of their pay.
- One who is not trustworthy with a little responsibility cannot be counted on to live up to a big responsibility. As such, employees should stay faithful even to the least of their responsibilities.
- A good employee will look for ways to advance the best interest of the company and will provide productiveness from the time their day commences until the close of business for the day.
- Knowing the status of one's performance helps them be a better employee by affording them the badly needed insight into what is working and what needs improvement.
- Objectivity is needed to ensure that appropriate criteria is established for measuring productivity and to make sure that subtle aspects of an employee's responsibilities are not overlooked in the process of creating their job description.
- It must be recognized that each person should possess a set of skills that serve as a tangible asset and each team must function as effectively as a machine.
- Teamwork is considered very critical to the success of the company and those individuals who once enjoyed star status are finding themselves outside the acceptable field of behavior.
- Jesus dealt with His disciples, clearly, fairly, and provided equitable recognition to them all.

Chapter 8 — Biblical Principles Versus Worldly Practices

As discussed in the previous chapter, following biblical principles can make a positive impact to the workplace and to the world. We are to differentiate the fruits of these biblical righteous principles with the worldly practices that often lead people into darkness and destruction.

Bible – the Corporate Turnaround Book

The dawn is eclipsed by the night
And corporations can't seem to do right
To regain the profits that they've lost
To energise the brands we love the most

But there is a light that shines to guide
Go through troubled times, with arms open wide
For the Bible has the lessons and the key
To guide your company to recovery

The lessons may seem unclear and hazy
But armed with faith, action and not being lazy
Can turn your corporation towards the light
And success, and profits will be in your sights

For the company is not a machine
Full of cogs, gears, and gasoline
But a living organism, that requires care
And a firm, healing hand, and the spirit to dare

With the Bible and a moral stance
You will avoid the devil's dance
And the pitfalls of greed and bankruptcy
And with good timing will promote harmony

Beware of False Shepherds

Most people around the world have heard of the devastating end that came to the followers of Jim Jones in the 1970's. More than nine hundred people took their own lives and killed their own children at the urging of a drug-addicted man who had convinced them that he was their only means to eternal salvation. This horrific event is a prime example of people allowing themselves to be blindly led by a person rather than studying Scripture on their own to become enlightened without undue influence.

Scripture warns against such situations and advises believers to test the fruits of teachers. Studying scripture enables us to discern the subject and the object of the message, which is a better way to learn the Word than to blindly accept what another person purports to be the truth. People will sometimes choose a topic and build a sermon around their topic, gleaning a little scripture here and there to support their oration.

In His infinite wisdom, within the pages of the bible, God has provided all the information humankind needs to lead a fulfilling life in the world. Though sometimes wrought with trials and tribulation, it is followed by the hope of an eternity in paradise. Jesus encouraged followers to learn the lessons found in scripture, empowering them to seek out the information that God wished for all of humankind to know without simply taking the word of their teachers. Jesus further taught humankind to test the fruit of the teachers and to practice discernment.

The Dangers of Blind Corporate Leadership

The practice of the blind leading the blind can creep into corporate practices as well. Management may lean too heavily on advice they receive from people who are more interested in achieving their own goals and ambitions than fulfilling the best interest of the corporation. Individuals who took advantage of their position to the detriment of everyone, including hardworking taxpayers, have plagued even governmental agencies. Whether the wrongful actions involve padding an expensive account, stealing materials and supplies, or even flagrant and criminal embezzlement, it is imperative that corporations maintain a set of checks and balances that preclude such activity. The real health of the company can be quickly damaged by irregularities in accounting that are deliberate such as in the recent cases of Enron and WorldCom.

No one who handles the corporate purse strings should be permitted to do so without having a trustworthy back-up looking over his or her shoulder. Maintaining tight controls over the financial status of any company is paramount to success, regardless of whether the company is a mom and pop business where they work out of their home, or a multi-billion dollar global enterprise. Even small infractions that violate the financial well-being can add up and rob the company of its badly needed operating capital. Every account should be assessed for signs of problems. The expense accounts of executives should be monitored for signs of excessive spending that might be personal rather than business related.

The bookkeeper should be able to produce a clean set of books that accounts for all money in and out of the corporation, backed up with receipts readily available to support the numbers. Employees, as well, should be able to account for supplies that are used, and evidence that equipment or materials are being lifted, should be investigated, and resolved. Respectful adherence to company policies is expected of everyone in the company.

The Fruits of Blind Shepherds May Include Glitz, Glamour and Lawsuits

In the 1960's a fledgling broadcasting network recruited a young couple to contribute to the growth of the network and they were elevated to star status in a short time. The variety type talk show of Jim and Tammy Faye Bakker were instrumental in building the initial success of the Christian Broadcasting Network. They also later became instrumental in helping Paul and Jan Crouch launch the Trinity Broadcasting Network with their famous program, "Praise the Lord". While that relationship only lasted for about a year, the Bakkers retained the rights to the program and took it to Charlotte, North Carolina where they launched The PTL Network. Then, in the early 1980's they built a Christian theme park, Heritage USA, which was the third most successful theme park in the United States at that time. Contributions received by their televangelist program were reported to be about one million dollars each week; and the Bakkers each earned six figure salaries and took multi-million dollar bonuses from the non-profit organization of which they were the figureheads.

Their lifestyle in the 1980's was one of flagrant excess. Then, in 1987, a sex scandal rocked the organization, when it was revealed that The PTL Network had paid off Bakker's former secretary, Jessica Hahn, to keep her from talking about her involvement with Jim Bakker. After Bakker resigned from PTL, accounting irregularities were discovered that exposed Bakker and his associates for selling lifetime memberships for three nights stay at a luxury hotel at Heritage USA to tens of thousands of people, in only a 500 room hotel, which had never been built. Jim Bakker actually raised enough money to build a hotel that would have accommodated the people who had bought the memberships, but reportedly kept much of the money for himself and used some of it to cover the expenses of operating Heritage USA. Later, after being convicted and having served five years in prison, Jim Bakker was released from prison early for good behavior. Three years later he was vindicated of the allegations that selling the hotel rooms had equated with selling securities by a Federal grand jury.

Over time, he has written books that attempt to explain the life of excess that led to the problems faced, and has openly admitted that it was only while he was imprisoned that he actually read the Bible all the way through. In one of his books, he explains that he had taken much of scripture out of context, which gave him the basis for living a life of such excessive consumption during the 1980's. Both Jim and Tammy Faye are still in considerable debt to the Internal Revenue Service, which revoked their non-profit status and applied sizable tax liens against them. Their actions and *behaviors seem to have stemmed from taking biblical*

96

teachings about prosperity to an extreme, and frequently using scripture out of context, which is not only inappropriate, but can be exceedingly harmful to the individual who does so, as well as others who may be impacted by their actions.

The Bakkers are not the only evangelists who have been involved in scandal. Numerous others have been convicted of criminal activity such as tax evasion, money laundering, mail fraud, embezzlement, and transporting stolen property across state lines. Some, who have not been convicted of crimes, have been publicly shamed through activities such as patronizing prostitutes, participating in drug abuse, being parties to lawsuits by people who had been taken advantage of in the name of ministry and evangelism.

Scripture exhorts that false shepherds will be known by their fruits. Many people have become famous, first appearing to be working on behalf of Christianity but later revealed to be wolves in sheep's clothes. Wisdom dictates that there will be those who are unable to resist the more seedy side of wealth and fame, but they should not be perceived to be a fair representation of Christianity.

Moral and upright Christians should know how to discern and recognize whether a ministry is producing good figs or bad ones.

Watching one's business closely for signs of bad figs may not be as easy as it would appear. People who will take advantage are often very charismatic, able to convince others that they are sincere and concerned for the welfare of the organization and every individual connected to it. If this were not true, most of the evangelists who have successfully spent years fleecing their flocks would not have gotten as far as they did.

In most cases where bookkeepers have been discovered embezzling funds from their boss, people would describe them as personable and unassuming, the last person you would expect to find involved in such an act. For this reason, it is important that a business found to be in a state of decline is well advised to call in an expert with the objectivity to look beyond the personal interactions that keep inappropriate deeds in the shadows. A corporate turnaround expert is able to uncover the source of the depletion whether it is related to unseemly activities or simply a matter of adjusting some of the business practices. Even in a healthy business, there is a constant need for adjustment to adapt to the changing times, to meet the needs of the customers, and to keep up with advancements in the given industry. Establishing a team whose purpose is to be watchful of the intricacies that are easily overlooked is both practical and prudent.

Upholding the Corporate Integrity

 Another effect that can be potentially harmful to a corporation is division among the ranks. All the various divisions and departments of the business must work together as a well-oiled machine. Failure to cooperate creates tension and discord that can lead to a decline in every facet of the corporation.

In the book of Revelation, the author wrote letters to the seven churches but only two of which met with full approval. The others needed to clean up some of their practices and were told exactly what they were doing wrong. His candid admonitions were important to insure that consistency and compliance with scriptural practices was maintained. In the corporate arena, this is important, too. A lack of cohesiveness creates a breakdown that will eventually impact the entire organization in a negative way. Studying the detailed information, Peter reveals that some of the churches were allowing paganism to infect the congregation. Dissension was disrupting the harmonious conduct of conveying God's message, and some members of the congregation were slack in their obligations. The messages about the churches are as insightful today as they were when they were written. Those desiring to do what is right will welcome the constructive criticism that can empower them to effect the necessary changes that could assure success.

Throughout the pages of the New Testament, the apostles provided clear guidance on conducts expected from believers. They warned Christians that immorality in the church would be judged. The attributes that were considered undesirable in the church are the same kinds of attributes that are harmful in the corporate world. Those who could be elevated to a position of authority and leadership in the church are expected to be reliable leaders of their own families. In his letters to Timothy, Paul described the kind of characteristics that should be sought for a bishop or a deacon in the church. Those characteristics include being vigilant, sober, of good behavior, hospitable, able to teach, not greedy, patient, and of pure conscience, among others. Those desiring a position of leadership in the church should possess many of the very same characteristics that are found in a competent business leader.

This principle explains why so many truly successful corporations are headed by CEOs who operate their business based on biblical principles. Additionally, most proficient corporate turnaround experts possess the qualities of character than cause them to seek the best interest of those they serve. That is one of the reasons they are able to achieve the kind of results that are needed to turn a corporation around. Providing a turnaround service to others and attempting to bring out the best in those being served requires a person who is wise, observant, and willing to serve. It requires honesty and diligence, sometimes in the face of opposition, to bring all the elements together and make them cohesive.

Conducting the early churches with a cohesive mission was sometimes difficult for the apostles. There were those who came into the church and wanted to restructure things to suit their own sense of what was ideal. Some wanted to incorporate doctrines that were not part of the gospel of Jesus and the apostles had to remain vigilant to watch out for those kinds of people. It was their intent that the teachings remain pure and true to the teachings of Jesus and the leading of the Holy Spirit. Many of the letters that Paul wrote to the various churches dealt with those issues, with constant warnings about avoiding misleading doctrines and practices.

Aside from Paul, Peter also exhorts the elders in the church to feed the flock, not by constraint as by lording leadership over the congregations, but by being a good example. He also exhorted the younger members to be humble.

More than the laws that Jesus came to fulfill, His stay on earth was a time for reestablishing the severed relationship with God among His people. He said that He is the way, the truth and the life[46]. He wanted his followers to see him as the fulfillment of the prophesy prophecy in the scripture.

Like Jesus, corporate leaders should also hold integrity in managing their posts. They should also be the first in the fulfillment of the corporation's vision, mission, and goals. They should show the right way in achieving those.

Key Learning Points:

- o Studying scripture enables us to discern the subject and the object of the message, which is a better way to learn the Word than to blindly accept what another person purports to be the truth.
- o The practice of the blind leading the blind can creep into corporate practices as well.
- o Maintaining tight controls over the financial status of any company is paramount to success.
- o Wisdom dictates that there will be those who are unable to resist the more seedy side of wealth and fame, but they shouldn't be perceived to be a fair representation of Christianity
- o Failure to cooperate creates tension and discord that can lead to a decline in every facet of the corporation.

Chapter 9 — Scriptural Practices Make Good Business Sense

If we are to see Jesus' presence on Earth millennia ago from a business perspective, He has established the greatest business that ever existed- Christianity. Moreover, He served as the best manager of all. His continuous and sincere teachings resulted in the successful venture of saving people from the prison of sinfulness.

Tradition Replaced with Truth

It may be difficult for some people to realize the correlation between religious organizations and corporate organizations, but truly there are more similarities than there are differences.

Christianity flourishes because it is ultimately headed by the greatest corporate turnaround expert of all time. Jesus was able to cause greater change in how people perceive God than all the kings, judges, and priest who had ever come before Him. People learned from Jesus that God is not inaccessible to the individual, that He is forgiving and long-suffering, that He desires a close relationship with His children, and that He is willing to make sacrifices for the sake of His children.

Jesus replaced the old tradition of people only attaining forgiveness through a priest, who was also himself a sinful person. He did this by offering Himself for the last time as the final blood sacrifice, thereby doing away with the need of offering sheep, goats, and bulls on alters. Because the veil that separated the Holy of Holies from the temple was torn from top to bottom the moment He died on the cross, Jesus opened the line of communication between Heaven and earth. This tearing away of the veil signified God's openness and paved the way for people to take their prayers directly to the Father. Jesus changed the

101

manner of practicing one's faith, first through His teachings, then through His sacrifice and later through the gospel message being carried into the world and spread through His apostles and followers. *The gospel message itself is life altering for people who absorb it and apply the teachings to their lives, making Jesus the most relevant expert on change that ever existed.*

Applying the gospel message to everyday life naturally translates to the way one conducts oneself in business, causing others to take notice. When someone turns his life to Christ, he becomes transformed and begins to look at things very differently. Old sinful behaviors lose their attraction. There may be internal struggles but working toward the goal eventually causes those struggles to decrease and Christian moral values come to the forefront. The desire to please God causes old behaviors like greed, envy, lust, and anger to be shed in exchange for behaviors like generosity, temperance, and kindness. People see the transformation and tend to make positive comments, which further reinforce the desire to maintain this way of life. The positive reinforcement also comes in the form of rewards like greater success, enhanced patience, contentment, and peace of mind. The result is more energy due to less struggle and better focus due to less inner turmoil. These feelings transport into the workplace where decisions become easier to make because they are taken with a greater awareness of purpose. The desire to serve others increases, causing a heightened sense of responsibility to make sober choices.

Applying these principles to corporate practices causes the business to run more smoothly and become more successful. Discarding the old ideas that businesses have to be ruthless and unscrupulous to survive is easy for a Christian who understands that it is possible to be competitive without degradation appearing. Competition is healthy and honorable as long as it does not cause harm to others. Aggressiveness is acceptable if it does not run roughshod over others, causing injury and conflict. Taking pride in one's work is not sinful as long as that pride is not a form of self-worship.

Jesus was a hard worker Himself, dedicated to working hard to get the message of the gospel to the masses in a short time. He traveled extensively, sacrificing His time and energy for the sake of fulfilling His mission. He upset the plans of those who did not conduct themselves according to the will of God by doing the will of God Himself. It made Him unpopular with some people and intensely desirable to others. He was neither intimidated by the ones who threatened Him, nor was He conceited over His popularity with those who loved Him. His heart was set on fulfilling His purpose on earth and He would not be stopped until that purpose had come to fruition. The power and authority of God was with Him and He was willing to complete the task He had come to accomplish knowing that the final price would be His death. However, He also knew and trusted that when He laid down His life He would be able to take it up again.

A Good Leader Exemplifies Patterns for Success

The ideas behind setting up the turnaround of a corporation suffering a state of decline are instilled in principles that follow the same patterns as those that established the advent of Christianity in the world. The first principle is that of installing a leader who has the vision and personal fortitude to undertake the task. As the book of Proverbs states, "Where there is no vision, the people perish[47]." If the leader is incompetent or inexperienced there cannot be a positive change in the state of conditions, but if the leader is intelligent, wise, and focused, there will be affirmative results.

Secondly, the problems that are causing the decline must be identified clearly. In a biblical sense, these problems are sinfulness and a lack of an appropriate relationship with God. In a business sense, the problems can be unbridled wrongdoing, inefficiencies, and ineffective workers. Once the problems are diagnosed, it is possible to prescribe an appropriate treatment and cure.

The bible identified the cure to be to send the Savior, Jesus Christ to establish the means for people to develop a right relationship with God. Of course, there is no worldly comparison to Jesus, and a business establishment is certainly not comparable with God. However, there is a similarity in that there must be a connection established between those who are involved in fixing the business problems and the entity that is the corporation. Someone must take the helm and be dedicated to the achievement of redirection. This individual must not be deterred from the task, regardless of the negative responses of those who are intimidated by the process. In any turnaround there will be individuals who will feel threatened and may attempt to sabotage the turnaround efforts in order to protect their own personal interest. That was the reaction of the religious leaders who were threatened by the teachings of Jesus; but, their attempts to quell the movement were unsuccessful because, as Gamaliel aptly stated, if the movement is of God, no man could overthrow it, and Christianity has not been overthrown.

The treatment program that is set up to accomplish a turnaround must be applied correctly and in a timely manner. In a biblical sense, one of the treatments was to perform the surgical removal of the unfruitful doctrines and practices that plagued humanity. The intermediaries who were obscuring the vision of salvation and blocking the path of those who longed for a close relationship with God severed. A healthy connection between God and humankind was established through Jesus and prevails through the present time by means of the Holy Spirit.

In a business sense, it may be necessary to eliminate practices that are counterproductive to the success of the corporation. This generally requires a cost analysis to determine where effective cuts can be made. Cost cutting may require closing down departments or division that fail to add value to the company. Creating savings may simply require the dismissal of individuals who are not productive. It may be necessary to replace long-standing relationships with vendors to give opportunity to vendors who provide better value for less money. Saving dollars may also mean severing relationships with customers with whom profitability was not truly being manifested.

The profitability factor is a critical one. Every account needs to be analyzed to determine the degree of profit that is being earned. Cost of goods or cost of services must be weighed against the income being generated. If the account is unfruitful, the customer can may be given the opportunity to make the business relationship profitable to the corporation. If they are unwilling or unable to do so, then it is vital that the ultimate decision to sever the relationship must be carried out. This is a hard decision, one that causes anguish and uncertainty; but if it is done in the light of replacing that account with a new customer who can bring a profitable account into the picture, then it is a positive step in the right direction.

Be Straightforward, Avoid Sugar- Coated Inaccuracies

Furthermore, in a turnaround process there are specific methodologies that need to be applied which are similar to those demonstrated by Jesus as He drew the masses to the new covenant with God.

Communication is crucial and not just in the sense of flinging out useless verbiage that fails to address the real issues. The communication must be honest and forthright, purposeful, and clear, providing those involved with the appropriate insight to empower them to comprehend their role in the turnaround process. While no one longs to hear bad news, the truth is more welcomed than useless dialog that fails to address the problem. In one turnaround process, the employees of the organization had become fed up with management that had been unable to address the problems that plagued the organization. The employees knew something was wrong, and though they had seen a turnover of management several times nothing positive ever transpired. When the turnaround expert was hired, he spoke to them candidly, advising them that the corporation was in trouble and that some of them might not be there in the months to come. Instead of disdain and resentment, he was met with a group of individuals who expressed relief that something was finally being done to repair the broken business. Instead of jumping off the ship, they got behind the effort and worked fervently to assist in the transformation. Honest communication, as conveyed in this example, was fundamental to fostering a sense of trust in the workforce. Though the news was bad news, it was concise and trustworthy rather than vague and sugar coated. Most intelligent people would rather be provided with truth, even if it is bad news, than to be given misinformation or no information at all. Truth is empowering, compelling those who know the truth to weigh their options and make decisions based on valid knowledge.

Enlist the Support of Everyone to Drive Success

Once communication has begun , it is possible to enlist the support of everyone who is impacted by the circumstances. When people are allowed to participate in the dialog surrounding the turnaround effort, ideas begin to flow. Knowing that their input may have an impact on the process, people who were once remiss about verbalizing their ideas will generally come forward with questions and suggestions that can be catalysts for turning the company around. The lack of confidence experienced by the workforce in the past will usually be replaced with a drive to contribute to the effort. *Turning the workforce into a real team can only be achieved if there is truthful communication between management and employees.*

Enlisting the support of His disciples was one of the first steps that Jesus took to begin His ministry. He was always open and truthful, instilling in them a sense of purpose. The example He set is one that can be emulated even in the business world. Moreover, Jesus maintained constant communication with God through prayer, always confirming that He was submitting to the will of God in all matters. He was straightforward in the dialog. He used to teach, to administer healing, to correct misunderstanding, and to rebuke the ones who were perpetuating wrongful practices and doctrines. Nothing less would have been effective.

By comparing this approach in communication to that within a corporate enterprise, one can see clear evidence that such truthfulness will make the communicator unpopular with some individuals. This response is to be expected, but should not be a deterrent. People cannot base their lives on lies, which is comparable to basing them on shifting sand, an analogy that was made by Jesus. People must be able to base their lives on a solid foundation of truth and trust.

Appropriate communication with customers is fundamental, too. While revealing too much information to them is not desirable, it is important to involve customers in the turnaround effort to assure them that the corporation is hard at work to fulfill its obligations to them. This applies as well to communicating with shareholders, also assuring them that their best interest is being looked into. Bankers, the government, and creditors must also be contacted and provided with proper information. However, the foremost task is that the workforce has the greatest leverage in exerting the actions that support the transformation. Enlisting the support of each entity concerned is vital but restraints must be used to avoid reactions of apprehension and dissension. While honesty is critical, a blatant outpouring of all the details about the problem is sure to cause alarm and will have a destructive effect. Prudent communication, on a need-to-know basis, will empower the turnaround team to enlist the support of the various parties involved in the process.

A No-Nonsense Approach to Management

Next, it is imperative to establish a no-nonsense approach to the management plan. As the preacher in the Book of Ecclesiastes told us, there is a time and season for all things. *Turning around the downward spiral of a struggling enterprise is not a time to inject comedy into the situation.* There is nothing funny about dragging a business out of the depths of despair. It is truly a serious undertaking, and must be handled as such. In order to be taken seriously, management must provide clear directives that promote the best interest of the recovery effort. Attempts to make the situation less stressful with humor may backfire because people need to remain focused on their tasks, and because they may not fully perceive the gravity of the circumstances if their manager is too jovial. Credibility must be maintained. It is best to save the comic relief for breaking the tension after strides have been made toward accomplishing the turnaround effort.

Additionally, management must be visibly prudent with expenditures during the turnaround effort while cutting costs.

Managers must not say one thing and do another. They must also adhere to the principles they establish and enforce. If corporate associates who travel are required to fly coach to save money, then the managers must not fly first class when they travel. They must not be dining in first class restaurants at the company's expense when the staff is retrenched to save cost. Cost cutting measures must be applied consistently and they must apply to everyone in the organization.

This was one of the most striking characteristics of Jesus and the disciples. They worked to earn their meals. Jesus ate with His disciples, sometimes providing food for the multitudes that gathered for His sermons, and He made good use of the resources they had at their disposal. They traveled by foot and stayed where they were invited to lodge, but always providing compensation to their host in some manner. Jesus set an excellent example of prudence and consistency that should be emulated by all managers, particularly those who have direct reports under their leadership.

Build a Solid Foundation by Concentrating on Core Competencies

An important aspect of establishing a turnaround is the need to concentrate on the core competencies of the corporation. During a rehabilitation process, it is important to remain vested in that which has been reliable and effective. This requires maintaining laser sharp focus on the task at hand. No one would want a surgeon to poke around haphazardly into their internal organs, or to operate on other patients simultaneously while attending their case; surgeons just do not do it that way. They care for one patient at a time, and only focus on the area that pertains to the surgery. In much the same way, following a highly focused course of action is critical to the success of the turnaround. When the goals have been established, and the path for achieving the goals has been laid out, staying on track is of vital importance because diversions can cause a breakdown of the plan.

Jesus profoundly demonstrated this concept in a number of ways. First, while He was in the wilderness, fasting and hungry, Satan approached Him and tried to tempt Him to turn stones to bread and feed Himself. However, Jesus rebuked him, telling him that man does not live by bread alone but by every Word of God. Then, when He came out of the wilderness, the devil tried to divert Him from His mission through various temptations, one of which was to offer Him all the kingdoms of the world if Jesus would bow down and worship him. However, Jesus responded by telling Satan that he must not tempt the Lord, and to follow Him[48]. At His weakest point, while He was hungry and exhausted, Jesus kept His focus on the mission that was before Him and would not be deterred. Through all the pain of being beaten, ridiculed, spat on and rejected, Jesus was steadfast and focused on His purpose. He continued to pray for those who subjected Him to the suffering, even with His dying breath.

Average people are not likely to be called on to exert the level of focus and dedication required to complete a mission so extreme. But much can be learned from examining the New Testament and studying Jesus' steadfast determination to reach the multitudes, as well as all the individuals who came to him in need. Keeping one's eye on the prize brings everything into perspective and prevents diversion of purpose.

In addition to staying focused on the core competencies, the corporation must be watchful to ensure that it only becomes involved with products and projects that are viable and profitable. While it may be tempting to take on projects that will boost the gross revenue of the corporation, the bottom line is to locate where the true value of the project must be evident from inception. Risk of loss, either through excessive costs to produce the project, or through an inability to collect from the customer, must be avoided. It is in the best interest of the corporation to turn down a project that will result in a loss. Merely having a contract is not enough; that contract must reap profits or it is merely a burden of time and energy that is better spent on work that provides real earnings. When calculating a bid on a contract or cost of goods to produce a product, there is a critical need to factor in a comfortable buffer to cover the inevitable contingencies that occur. Expect the markets that support the project or the product to escalate in cost and realize that the estimates of prices for materials and supplies may be markedly higher by the time the work commences.

Making those kinds of allowance provides breathing room in the event if there is a sudden spike in cost of goods during the course of completing the contract. When the contract becomes a sure thing, approach vendors and ask for contracted prices on the materials and supplies that you will purchase within specified time-frames. This will help to ensure that your costs will not escalate before you complete the project. Do not hesitate to ask for discounts based on quantities or for paying within a certain time period. Some vendors are often happy to provide discounts that they do not necessarily publicize. The answer may be no but it is better to ask just in case the answer is yes. It would be imprudent to overlook an opportunity to save money. Exploring every potential avenue to make contracts more valuable will insure that you are not creating liabilities in the quest to boost the earnings of the corporation.

Challenge Past Assumptions to Avoid Idolizing a Sacred Cow

Another important aspect of negotiating the right direction in a turnaround effort is to challenge past assumptions about what works or not. In this rapidly changing world the one thing that is certain is change, and it is critical to avoid getting stuck in a rut. A corporation will often find a successful product and will focus entirely on that product, overlooking other potentially viable products that could be added to their line of merchandise. Such a product is often referred to as a cash cow.

A business in this position runs the risk of allowing their cash cow to become a sacred cow, which can lead to having it turn into a mad cow. This generally leads to trouble, just as the Israelites got into trouble when they became impatient to have something to worship and ended up worshiping a golden calf, much to the distress and angst of Moses. From a biblical perspective, idol worship has always led to God's displeasure and has caused entire nations to fall. From a business perspective, idolizing a particular product to the exclusion of considering other viable products can also lead to demise of a company.

110

Build a Budget that Works, Instead of Working for a Budget

Turning a corporation around is often a very complicated process, which requires prudent budgeting, and tight financial constraints. It is wise to adopt a zero budget base and carefully increase it by small amounts. Controlling costs is vital to the success of even the healthiest corporation but when one is faced with a sick corporation, this factor becomes even more imperative.

Some corporations that are in a downturn might have to face one or more major financial considerations in order to pull out of a recessive situation. The most dramatic, and often the one that gets primary consideration are downsizing. This will certainly save the business money in the short term but it may not be the most advisable stance to take. While downsizing can be necessary in the event of a merger or the loss of a major customer, it can sometimes actually hurt a corporate recovery more than it will help. However, if downsizing is unavoidable, it must be done carefully.

While it is wise to trim the fat and letting go of the personnel that provides the least amount of support to the organization, great care must be taken to avoid pouring off the cream, :the best and most supportive personnel. This is an area where great attention is required to ensure that all divisions and departments are adequately covered for the smooth continuation of business.

Losing critical personnel during a restructuring process is one of the greatest natural risks there is. There is no point in inadvertently dismissing the highly motivated people who are willing to stick it out. Instead, look for the 'malignant' personnel. These are the ones who are not only unproductive but who are also somewhat toxic to the process and the organization. These are the people who complain and demoralize the associates around them. Sometimes a downturn can be a good opportunity to clean house and trim the staff down to eliminate the people who were a drain on everyone else. *Again, it bears reiterating that downsizing should not necessarily be the first reaction to a downturn.*

111

A good first reaction is to examine the corporate budget carefully to look for areas that can tolerate budget cuts without interfering with production or productivity. Look for ways to reduce the fixed and variable operating overhead that still allows for the uninterrupted servicing of customers. Look for assets that may be sitting idle and determine whether there is a way to make them useful to generate viable income. If not, they are fair game for liquidation. Do not keep an unused piece of equipment around in the hope that you will one day find a purpose for it, sell it to someone who can use it, and apply the cash to purposeful use in your recovery. Control your inventory levels and avoid allowing items to build up that may become obsolete instead of generating revenue. Watch all your departments carefully and establish an auditing system that permits you to have a real time look at your financial status. Review your standing contracts, with vendors and customers, and renegotiate the terms whenever you can to give your cash flow the edge. Consider simple changes that can add up to big differences in the long run, such as energy usage within your facility. Encourage employees to come up with cost saving suggestions that pertain to their departments. However, when cutting costs, do not compromise the quality of the product or service, prudent use of resources, and eliminating waste can often yield better results than you might anticipate. Taking these measures establishes a pattern that you will want to continue even after solvency has returned to a comfortable level.

Jesus Worked With Nearly Nothing yet He Had Everything He Needed

It is interesting to note that Jesus operated His organization with no assets, no office, and no mode of transportation. Yet, He traveled extensively and always had food and drink. He made mention to His disciples and followers that they should not worry about what they would wear or the food they would eat. He noted that the lilies neither toil nor plant, yet they are beautifully clothed. He reminded His followers many times that God provides for the needs of those who have faith in Him. Clearly, He demonstrated that His faith in God could turn a few loaves of bread into enough to feed a multitude.

Using the meager resources He had at His disposal, Jesus started a movement that has continued for more than twenty centuries. Faith, Work, and Grace has transformed the world from a dark place where sin prevailed unbridled, and those lost in it oblivious to its grip on them, to a world that has been brought into the light, due to the teachings of Christ. With present-day enlightenment we are feeding, clothing and housing more people than any civilization that has come before. There is still much work to be accomplished, but the compassion and generosity that the world learned because of Jesus has made mankind more humane. He did all this with a very limited amount of worldly possessions, setting a remarkable example for making the most of what one has. The world was a very different place back then; but even the most modest of individuals of that time had more than He did. He willingly gave up a heavenly habitation to visit the world, with no possessions to call His own, all to the achievement of giving life to humanity, and that life being one of abundance. He valued what He had, those lost sheep He came to shepherd, the lost souls He came to find.

Key Learning Points:

- o Jesus served as the best manager of all. His continuous and sincere teachings resulted in a successful venture of saving people from the prison of sinfulness.
- o The gospel message itself is life altering for people who absorb it and apply the teachings to their lives, making Jesus the most relevant expert on change that ever existed.
- o Applying the gospel message to everyday life naturally translates to the way one conducts itself in business, causing others to take notice.
- o The desire to serve others increases, causing a heightened sense of responsibility to make sober choices
- o Jesus was a hard worker Himself, dedicated to working hard to get the message of the gospel to the masses in a short time.

In an business enterprise :

o The profitability factor is a critical one. Every account should be analyzed to determine the degree of profit that is being earned.
o The communication must be honest and forthright, purposeful and clear, providing those involved with the appropriate insight to empower them to comprehend their role in the turnaround process.
o An important aspect of establishing a turnaround is the need to concentrate on the core competencies of the corporation.
o Controlling costs is vital to the success of even the healthiest corporation but when one is faced with a sick corporation, this factor becomes even more imperative.
o Next, examine other financial parameters, which will give an indication of the corporate health to include growth in sales and profits, gross margin, profitability, return on sales, return on capital etc.

Chapter 10— Growing Out of a Downturn and Into Success

Many businesses that were successful in the past but suddenly faced with a downturn, have the tendency to just sell out or accept the fate of a bankruptcy. However, there are some that have recovered from a downturn by applying a better approach to doing business — the approach used by Jesus, the corporate turnaround expert.

Beyond Resuscitation - Striving to Revitalize and Renew

Up to this point, much has been written about what to do in order to pull the corporation out of a downturn. These elements have focused on the resuscitation of the corporation, fundamentally to achieve a more liquid cash flow and to reposition the corporation to operate more efficiently. *However, resuscitation is only one of the steps and will not sustain the long-term viability of the business.* Often, when the recovery phase of a turnaround has been completed, managers will stop the turnaround process and expect the corporation to revitalize itself. However, running a corporation requires an ongoing effort to maintain its state of good health. This can be compared to taking vitamins to strengthen the body's resistance to infection. *There must be an ongoing process that preserves the well-being of the company. That process is revitalization and renewal.*

The revitalization process is imperative to promote the healthy growth of a corporation that has been involved in a recovery effort. Revitalization is a succession that follows the recovery phase to propel the corporation from a state of merely being functional to that of being a thriving, growing, and dynamic entity. It requires the use of a complex set of concepts that surpass those used for resuscitation. It involves the implementation of an aggressive marketing strategy, the willingness to take risks, and the development of a strong, healthy corporate culture.

Unlike the resuscitation phase, which required focus on healing the unhealthy practices of the corporation, revitalization is a strengthening process for the purpose of making the corporation more powerful and assertive. It can be compared to physical therapy and exercise that a doctor might prescribe following major surgery. The exercises are necessary to restore healthy blood flow throughout the body and physical therapy is necessary to insure that all the body parts work correctly and in unison.

Revitalization can further be compared to the gospel message that Jesus brought to the world, which was further spread by His followers. Clearly, the old religious practices were not providing the close personal relationships between God and His children. When Jesus came into the world to debunk the unscriptural doctrines and practices that held people back, He did not merely cut out the old traditions that served to block their relationship with God. He continued the process into the revitalization of their commitment to living a life that would be pleasing to God. He equipped them with a new covenant, one that renewed their faith and provided them with an unprecedented ability to approach God with their prayers and supplications. He presented them with fresh ideas, a deeper understanding of what was truly expected of them, and the assurance that God was a loving Father who desired what was best for them. He debunked the notion that God was vengeful and wrathful toward them, ready to punish them for every infraction. Jesus provided them with the insight that what God truly desired from them was repentance and acceptance of the values He had introduced through the Ten Commandments.

The creation of the new covenant included His teaching and development of the high-level followers, those being the twelve apostles, who would continue to carry forth this message. The act of setting up the revitalization of belief in God involved enormous risk-taking, including rejection. He was rejected by some, which ultimately led Him to the cross. However, this was not the end of His work. His message had already piqued the interest and desire of so many people that when He was resurrected and revealed Himself to His disciples, assuring them that He would send the Holy Spirit to lead them, they were ecstatic. Thus, the renewal of their faith empowered them to set out to continue to spread the gospel, and it is still being spread to this day. *Christianity is now the world's largest corporate entity, having been born of the most humble of beginnings.*

While no man has the power and authority of Christ to lay down such a broad foundation, it is possible to emulate the values He conveyed and to integrate those values into the way one conducts their business. It is even advisable, to take the effort to a higher level, one which involves a spiritual infusion into the process. It is one thing to conduct oneself in a manner that is pleasing to humankind, and yet another to strive to please God. Therefore, if the ultimate objective is to live and work in a manner that is pleasing to God, the choices and actions made by an individual are more likely to be successful and well-founded.

While the corporation itself cannot have faith, those who run the corporation can choose to apply practices that are in agreement with the commandments of God. Introducing this spiritual approach to the revitalization process is truly the best medicine to insure a healthy future.

At the forefront of revitalization is, as mentioned earlier in this section, formulating a highly aggressive marketing approach. There are actually four different aspects of forming the marketing approach, and while they all have some level of merit, one of the four is particularly vital.

The first approach is an internal marketing strategy, one that is based on sales figures and product costs. While these figures are important and certainly play a pertinent role in developing the marketing strategy, they are not enough on their own.

The next approach is a competitor based marketing strategy, one that is based on the trends being followed by the competition. While it is important to consider the influence of the competition, this strategy alone will actually cause the corporation to crash into obstacles that were unforeseen because of excessive focus spent on examining competitors.

Another marketing strategy is one that is customer based, centered on fulfilling the demands of the customer. Certainly, it is important to please the customer and to fulfill their needs but basing a marketing strategy entirely on the premise of meeting customer demands is not only ineffective, it is dangerous. Customer demands change continually and no corporation can keep pace with them in a real time sense. Attempting to do so will leave the corporation in a state of utter despair.

However, there is one marketing strategy that is not only effective, it is progressive enough to propel the corporation into a high level of success. The market driven approach to the corporate marketing strategy is powerful and insightful. It is an approach based on vision and anticipation. This approach requires an analysis of customer and competitor trends, evaluation of the marketplace and calculations that project the direction of new markets. Using this strategy empowers the corporation to develop the right product for the times, and to apply the correct pricing to the product, one based on both cost of production and an understanding of what the market will bear.

A prime example of successfully tapping into the market driven strategy is CNN News, which was cajoled by other broadcast companies at its inception. However, Ted Turner was insightful enough to see that the consumer marketplace was in need of a twenty-four hour news program, and today CNN is one of the most powerful broadcast agencies in the world. It points to the fact that it is imperative to truly understand the market one is attempting to satisfy. This requires doing a lot of homework, including research and analysis of customer trends, and requirements.

Likewise, part of what has made Dell Corporation so successful is their ability to meet customer needs on a personal level, as opposed to expecting the customer to resolve their needs to accept an out-of-the box product. While this may sound like it is totally a customer driven approach, it is in reality more in the realm of being market driven by virtue of the fact that the personal computer industry is highly diverse. Dell's success lies largely in the fact that it is able to meet the diverse needs of its customers through unparalleled flexibility with consistency and timeliness. Meeting the marketplace expectations is easier when products are developed based on aggressive pursuit of the market driven strategy.

Educate the Workforce to Create a Powerful Asset

Another element fundamental to successful revitalization is the appropriate development of the staff. This will generally involve integrating basic training with ongoing educational programs for managers and workers that are pertinent to their job requirements.

Managers should be educated with the concepts of personnel recruitment, retention, and development. They should understand how to analyze data related to their department and how to make adjustments based on that analysis. Workers should be well trained and educated in the latest technology related to their jobs. Proper training provides them with the foundation needed to perform required tasks with knowledgeable efficiency. While untrained workers are a liability, well-trained workers are a tangible asset; and those who undergo continuing education become wellsprings of ideas that benefit the company on a scale that is immeasurable.

Many of the best ideas launched as products or services by numerous corporations have come from members of the workforce. Keeping them on a steady diet of resources and information promotes the well-being of the entire corporation. Some corporations have created initiative programs whereby they reward workers who formulate ideas that end up in the marketplace. They generally reward them through bonuses and recognition. Many of the patents held by corporations are for intellectual property or a product that was the brainchild of a shrewd employee, one who created a process that not only benefited the employer, but which also empowered the company to retain exclusive rights to use the process or create the product. Additionally, employees who receive proper training and ongoing education tend to be more confident, likely to persevere, and more likely to be retained.

This brings us to another exercise in the revitalization process, which progresses to a higher level than merely training and educating the employees and managers. This exercise is one that strengthens the corporation overall because it entails drawing on the energy of the workers. Employees who are adequately trained

119

and committed to the revitalization effort are easy to get excited about the prospect of a promising future with the corporation. If they are provided with vital feedback concerning the value of their contribution to the corporation, it feeds their energy level and heightens their sense of morale. *Recognition and accolades are like vitamin therapy for the workforce and are proven to be more effective to enhance productivity* than only receiving negative feedback for shortcomings.

Meetings can become vibrant with an energetic exchange of ideas, many of which may easily end up becoming viable projects. People tend to be very passionate about their ideas and the result is that their passion can be converted into drive and productivity. Promoting an open, free flowing exchange of ideas has a positive impact on the corporation, as has been well demonstrated by such companies as Disney, Google, and Oracle.

A healthy company will consume three meals a day, those being 'vision for breakfast, feedback for lunch, and action for dinner'. Vision provides a clear image of the preferable future of the corporation; feedback is critical input based on the stated vision; and action involves making a decision and moving forward. These three meals are each equally important and none of them should be skipped. Each provides a different form of nourishment for the company and none of the three is adequate solely on its own.

Just as a corporation focuses on vision, feedback, and action, Jesus did also. He cast His vision for humanity to His disciples. The passion behind His vision was evident and contagious. Once the disciples understood the vision, they could not be stopped in helping Jesus accomplish it. When there were issues where they lacked a clear understanding of the vision, Jesus talked with them and allowed time for feedback. In addition, Jesus was a man of action. The Gospel in the bible is packed with examples of the actions Jesus took to accomplish His vision.

Development of corporate culture through training, recognition, and encouragement will create an atmosphere that is positively charged. Ideas and information will begin to flow through the organization, providing more opportunities to develop new products and better ways to serve customers. *Keep in mind that ideas and information are both useless unless action is taken to put them to work. Innovation is an essential component to the revitalization process*, providing a means to introduce exciting new products or services to customers.

It is important for your customers, creditors, and shareholders to see the fruits of the corporation's advancements being introduced to the market. Learning to drive the market through the introduction of innovative products or services is easier when the culture of the corporation is receptive to employee input. The staff members who deal first hand with customers often receive input that is vital to the development of better offerings for the market. Those employees should have the means to move the information they obtain through proper channels so that it gets into the hands of the people responsible for project development. Each department in the organization should be gleaning and gathering information that can be taken into consideration. The information has to be sifted and weighed for its value, but unless it is collected in the first place, it has no value.

Sometimes it is not feasible or manageable to produce everything that goes into creating a product or a service. It may be easier in some cases to locate a vendor that can take on some aspect of creating a product or providing a service. Outsourcing has gained popularity simply because it is frequently the most cost effective and easiest way to get a product to market. If it is cost prohibitive to develop a product due to the cost of outfitting a production plant, look into the viability of sending out that portion of the work to a vendor who is already outfitted with the proper equipment. Be sure to bind vendors into comfortable contracts that protect your intellectual rights, prohibiting them from sharing information about your product with others. However, when you find a vendor who can assist you in producing your product, you may reap incredible benefits as a result of the relationship. *Expanding through outsourcing can often help the corporation produce more at a greater savings than you will realize from buying more equipment and hiring more people yourself.*

At the time Jesus was teaching His disciples, preparing them for His imminent death that only He knew was coming, He took great pains to ensure that they were prepared to carry the gospel message on His behalf. He also used them to convey His energy and power to affect the miraculous healings of those who were sick, lame, blind, or possessed among the multitudes. Functioning in this manner allowed Him to reach more people,

121

more quickly and gave His disciples the confidence to carry out His purpose, even in His absence. The power of God was manifested through the disciples because they were well prepared to be used in that manner. Jesus consistently encouraged them and made good use of their energy. Jesus understood the importance of improving the quality of life for the needy and His ministry on their behalf brought glory and honor to God. He had essentially outsourced His power to a team He trusted and it was fully to the benefit of those who received His mercy. Everyone involved benefited from the experience.

Another fundamental aspect that is critical to the revitalization of a corporation is the willingness to accept new ideas. This idea does not oppose the need to concentrate on the core competencies; rather it is an enhancement to that ideology. While using the solid foundation of focusing on what works, it is advisable to pursue ideas that can be complementary to that which is already known to be viable. *If the old way of doing things is becoming outmoded, look into newer technology or better processes that allow the corporation to function more efficiently.* Fortunes have been made on new ideas and new methodologies, so avoid dismissing new idea as impertinent until they have been investigated. In evoking the use of new ideas, the corporation must be willing to accept failure. *Failure should not be perceived as a sign of defeat instead as a lesson in what not to do in the future.* Before dismissing the idea that failure can be okay, consider the fact that most major corporations have suffered failure at one time or another in their histories. However, that does not mean the corporation should throw all caution to the wind.

The willingness to accept failure as a result of innovation must be based on a reasonable comfort level. Because of having come through the resuscitation phase, there should be a comfort level that already exists by the time the company is working on revitalization. The old saying goes "Nothing ventured, nothing gained"; so venture into some unfamiliar territory but do it with valid information and due consideration. Take care, but explore new initiatives that might lead the corporation into the level of success that is desired. Keep in mind that timing is important, so if a new proposal comes forth, be sure to give it proper consideration quickly to avoid having a competitor beat you to it. Most of the products that are in use today were introduced at just the right time to spark the interest of consumers, so never forget that timing is everything.

Jesus certainly arrived in the world in a timely manner. The Roman Empire was spreading out and taking possession of areas of the world that had previously been very disconnected. Judaism was the primary religion in Jerusalem and the surrounding areas, but Rome ruled the land. There were relationships with Greece and Egypt, which meant that travel and freedom of movement was relatively unencumbered. He was born at the time that Herod the Great was ruling and lived into the Caesarian era. Judaism enjoyed freedom of worship, relatively unhindered by the government. Because of the mode of government, the religious leaders could not prevent Him from preaching the gospel and He was able to spread His message to many people very quickly. It took great effort on the part of the religious leaders to find a reason to bring Him before Pilate just prior to the crucifixion, and afterward, His apostles were able to hold meetings that broadened the expanse of Christianity throughout the world. Certainly, God had chosen this time carefully as being the right time in history for His Son to come into the world in the flesh. Regardless of why God chose the particular time He did, the arrival of Christ certainly yielded a harvest that continues to grow in its bounty. He came into the world with an unprecedented attitude of determination to turn the hearts of the children towards the Father in Heaven.

An Attitude of Determination Replaces Negative Practices

In order to achieve true progress, there must be a positive attitude prevailing through every stage of the process. A good way to nurture a healthy attitude is through the maximization of positive corporate values and operating through a best practices program. Keep a close eye on finances and make sure that every department is operating within its budget. Timely information permits the corporation to respond quickly if finances seem to be a little off the mark. Watching for practices that are highly efficient and striving to emulate those practices is cost effective.

Discerning which practices are ineffective and finding better methods will reap more benefits. Instill in everyone an attitude of nurturing the company, teach them to care for it as if it was their very own, and success will be forthcoming. Negative attitudes must be dealt with before they have a chance to adversely impact the corporation.

The negative attitudes of the chief priests and Pharisees were always dealt with in a forthright manner. Jesus demonstrated great authority, knowledge and a purity of conscience that put them in their place each time they confronted Him. He knew that His purpose was greater than their practices. He knew that His faith was more important than their doctrines. He had already told His disciples that He would lay down His life for His flock, and that this would be done willingly. He made it known to them that no one had the power to take His life without His consent. His resolve to comply with the plan of God reflected His positive attitude about the purpose of His visit to the world. He was fully committed to the plan, and none of the religious leaders would be able to stop the spread of the gospel once His purpose was fulfilled. He had related to the masses in a way that no one ever had, and they considered it a privilege and a great honor to continue to spread His message. Christians today carry that same attitude; their salvation through grace makes them want to share the message that Jesus is Lord.

This brings up another important aspect of revitalizing a corporation. It is important to instill in the customers a sense of loyalty and commitment. The best and most reliable form of advertising for any corporation is by word of mouth. Customers who extol the virtues of a product or a service have more advertising leverage than any other means of reaching new customers. In order to increase sales, induce in your present customers a desire to become evangelists for your company. If one customer tells two people, who each tell two more people, sales will grow exponentially without the corporation having to spend a single dollar on advertising. This is not to imply that a good marketing strategy is not vitally important. That aspect was already discussed earlier in this text, but when the aggressive marketing plan has done its job, a great deal then rides on the contentment of the customer. Be sure that your product or service will truly live up to its purpose so that customers will give you accolades instead of throwing rotten tomatoes at your facility. In the same way that word of mouth can boost sale when customers are very pleased, badmouthing from customers can be devastating. The sad reality is that fewer happy customers will spread good news about your product or service compared to the displeased ones who are louder and who will spread bad news.

Vietnam Payment Technologies Joint Stock Company (VinaPay) is an example of a customer-focused company. The nature of the company's services really requires that it should get the trust of its customers. Its vision reads that the company is dedicated as a leader in payment solutions through innovation and commitment to their customers. It is also committed in maintaining a perfect customer services culture and bringing comprehensive development for all its stakeholders and customers.

A good way to insure great customer relations is to follow up with your customers. Ask for their feedback and put that feedback to good use. You can do this in a number of ways and they are all reliable for gathering customer satisfaction data. You may wish to send out a card with a product for them to fill out and send back. Some corporations send out a sheet inviting the customer to log in and give feedback on a website. Perhaps you may prefer to have customer service representatives follow up with a phone call. Either way, *gathering responses from customers is a proactive way to permit your customers a channel through which they can reach you with their thoughts, feelings, and suggestions regarding your product or service.* Collecting this vital information is relatively easy and lets the corporate analysts and managers gain greater insight into the needs of the people the corporation is trying to serve. Statistically speaking, many will not respond, but others will, and you can get a good cross section through which you can develop a rating of how satisfied your customers are overall.

Another vital aspect to the success of a corporation deals with collecting receivables from customers. Many companies have become so weighed down with uncollected receivables that they were rendered unable to pay their own bills. Caution should be exercised in the extension of credit in the first place. However, when extending credit to customers it is vital to ensure that their payments are flowing in within a timely manner. Some corporations feel that it is better for customer relations to offer a discount for payment in advance or within a specified number of days, as opposed to penalizing customers with interest for late payments. Both methods are used, but offering discounts usually keeps the cash flow of the corporation more liquid than assessing interest on balances, so discounts are very popular. Most companies actually use both methods of encouraging prompt payments on their account receivables, and since it is the business norm, customers tend to expect it to be that way. Do not feel badly about asking a customer to pay a higher rate of payment if they withhold payment over a specified time; your bankers do not feel badly about charging you interest. In addition, the discounts will not be damaging if you make allowance in your pricing. Most companies have discount programs for customers who purchase high quantities and the amount of the discount for expedited payment should fall within similar parameters. Additionally, offering discounts is another means of establishing good customer relations and insuring satisfaction. Regardless of how the corporation chooses to address this issue, collecting receivables is the lifeblood of the corporation and attention to doing so should receive very high priority.

Paying accounts payable in the manner you hope to collect your receivables is another way to insure smooth conduct of your business. Paying your vendors and suppliers in a timely manner increases the likelihood that you will not be hit with delays in obtaining the materials and supplies needed to conduct your business. Failure to pay those bills on time may create ill will and will certainly cause those creditors to delay shipments that you need, to produce your merchandise or continue your service. *Take advantage of discounts they may offer, but do not overload your inventory by using excessive quantity discounts.* Avoid incurring interest on accounts payables because this increases the cost of producing goods and services, making your profits go down.

Accounting requires a great balancing act because the overall concept is maintaining a state of healthy cash flow. It is critical that the entire accounting department functions cohesively. Frequent audits of accounts can prevent surprises from cropping up and adversely affecting the corporation financially. Be sure that tax payments are made as required, that there is adequate funding to cover payroll, and that money is flowing in at a rate that surpasses the outflow. Audit inventory levels often to make sure that too much of one thing is not being kept on hand while you are running out of another. Materials required for production should never run out, because you may end up with stopped production lines that are costing you money by virtue of the fact they are stalled. This situation tends to create a snowball effect because late production translates into arriving late to market, which in turn causes disgruntled customers. The accounting department simply must run smoothly, using reliable checks and balances that protect the corporation from any likelihood of misinterpreting its financial status.

Furthermore, when assessing the financial status of the corporation, keep in mind that cash flow, receivables and payable, inventory, and cost of goods are only a part of the big picture. Assets and capital investments are also pertinent to establishing the true value of the company, and those items are a form of leverage for financing in times of expansion, or in the worst case scenario, brief periods of minor distress. Ideally, a corporation will maintain a capital fund for the purpose of business expansion or dealing with unexpected emergencies, but sometimes it may be necessary to seek outside financing. While it is very unhealthy to borrow money to cover day-to-day operations, it is imperative that the corporation maintain an up-to-date financial statement and balance sheet in the event it does need to borrow money from a lending institution. As stated, borrowed money is best used for developing innovative new products, or to enable the corporation to extend a service that will generate new revenue, and in every instance that it is used, it should be paid back promptly.

There are a myriad of other details that are pertinent to the turnaround process. The situation of each entity is unique so there is no simple, 'out-of-the-box' solution that will work for everyone. Because of the complexity of operating a corporation, even under the best of circumstances, it is very important to use the elements outlined in this book to personalize a process that is appropriate for the corporation to which it pertains. Inviting the professional services of a turnaround expert can help to minimize the complexity, making it a less menacing task. Whether the expert is brought on board for a long term or simply as a consultant for a short time, the immeasurable value of the services of such an expert can make a big difference in the outcome. Since no entity is truly defeated until it accepts defeat, there is hope for re-establishing the corporation, even a good chance of making it better and stronger than ever. Achieving the desired goal requires consistent and unrelenting effort with constant attention to details.

Human spirituality is very closely tied to the way people function, at work and away from work. Managers have often been confronted with uncomfortable scenarios because they have been called on to make decisions about matters that conflict with their spiritual nature. Knowing where to turn in those times is important for alleviating the stress and anguish associated with matters that violate their faith. Prayer and sincere faith that God is there and that He truly cares, is a powerful means of coping with the difficulties that life presents. The desire to live a life pleasing to God, coupled with a genuine effort to do so, empowers the individual to make decisions and to take action with greater clarity of conscience. Applying the biblical principles to every aspect of one's life provides trustworthy reference points that ward off turmoil. The bible defines appropriate methods of dealing with conflict and proper ways of relating to others in the workplace, as well as with one's family. Jesus taught us to be kind to one another and to forgive. He taught us that it is honorable to work to the best of our ability and to provide employers an honest day of work for our pay. He taught that employers should be kind to their workforce and provide them with pay appropriate to the task. The bible teaches that if someone will not work, neither should they eat; but, if someone cannot work because of an infirmity , then they should be cared for by the church. The bible teaches that we should exercise self-control, moderation in all things, and above all else, reverence for God. Prosperity hinges on making good choices with due consideration on how our choices will have an impact on the people and the world around us.

Create New Products and Innovate

Thomas Edison was said to have tried over ten thousand different materials in his quest for a filament that would make his light bulb work. Henry Ford's engineering team failed repeatedly to create the design for the V-8 engine before they hit on a design that worked. IBM turned down Bill Gates' proposals several times before the latter established his computing empire. Long successful, Coca-Cola Corporation even suffered a major failure in its introduction with New Coke, eventually scraping the project and reviving its well established formula for success. Therefore, if your business has suffered setbacks, disappointments, even failure in some endeavor, then you can consider yourself in good company. Not every idea is going to evolve into a successful product or service but that doesn't mean you stop formulating ideas. Not every product is going to be met with rave reviews but some will, so you can't give up on creating new products.

The best insurance against failure is doing your homework. The Internet is inundated with agencies that conduct consumer opinion polls. Research agencies have already done a lot of the homework for the industrial sector and their findings are published, available to business leaders for prices that range from free to the thousands of dollars. As mentioned earlier, consumer feedback from existing customers is a great tool that inspires the advancements of many corporations who take advantage of its merit. Numerous other methods of compiling information exist that provide valid and timely statistics to help you understand your customers better.

Employ a Holistic Approach for a Healthy Outcome

Just as a doctor often prescribes a combination of treatment to create a holistic plan of care for a sick patient, a corporate turnaround expert will prescribe a plan of care for a sick corporation.

From a biblical perspective, Jesus arrived as the Great Physician to heal a sick world, offering a type of lifestyle that would lead to better health of the soul. His teachings did not stop with His sacrifice at the cross but still continue to this day through the Holy Bible. Learning the significance of the parables and lessons Jesus taught can clarify some of the cloudy issues pertaining to living a life of abundance.

Abundance is not always measured in the amount of money or the number of possessions one has; instead, abundance refers to a holistic quality of life that cannot be measured in dollars or things. Jesus once said that His yoke was light and His burden was easy; and considering that there are billions of Christians, there are clearly a lot of people who agree with Him. The burden of sin certainly is heavy and hard to bear, not merely because of the threat of a wrathful judgment, but fundamentally because it causes hardship.

Running a major corporation should not be a constant hardship. Of course, there will be times things will not run smoothly, but that should be the exception instead of the norm. After the turnaround of a corporation has been effectively achieved, it becomes vital to follow up with preventative measures to keep the business running efficiently. Just as a person should go to the doctor for wellness checkups, a corporation should also undergo wellness checks. It is much easier to maintain a healthy state of existence than to recover from sickness. Many of the same strategies that applied to the recovery effort should be integrated into the methodologies used to keep the corporation running at optimum performance.

Likewise, living in a manner that conforms to the spiritual values emulated in scripture is healing for someone who suffers from a broken spirit. Consistent application of biblical values helps to ward off spiritual turmoil because there are answers for all of life's questions found within the pages of the bible. Anguish is replaced with hope, sorrow is replaced with joy, and uncertainty is replaced with assurances of God's love and concern for all of humankind. The stories in the bible are vivid depictions of the vast difference between the way of life is with God as opposed to life without Him. However, a careful examination of the text reveals more than simple stories of biblical figures; within those stories are lessons about life that demonstrate poignant truths about our purpose and God's plan for humankind.

There are lessons about ways to treat others, how to gain God's favor, what is expected in return for favor, and ways to deal with everyone from creditors to tax collectors. Ernest searching for truth reveals the truth, first as milk and later as meat, for the Word of God is nourishment for the soul. Jesus has been called Living Water because He alone has the ability to quench our thirst for knowledge that will sustain us now and in the future.

He has been called the Bread of Life, and truly, His lessons fill us with nourishing enlightenment. He has the power and ability to remove us from paths of destruction that lead to certain death of our spirit, and He can place us on a path that is flooded with His light so that we are able to clearly see where we are going.

The Key to Achieving Victory is Surrender

To invoke the power to turn one's life around and ultimately to turn one's business to prosperity, there is only one major requirement - surrender. Surrender to the yoke of Jesus, which He said would be easy, and the burden would be light. One needs only to surrender to the Word of God, surrender to the truth about creating a fruitful life and even to the real truth about what a fruitful life really is in the first place. More than two billion people have surrendered to the Lord, some totally and some tentatively, but in the end most who embark on a path of spiritual enlightenment find that though they suffer trials and tribulations just as everyone else does, they have one thing that others cannot claim. They have immeasurable hope that they will overcome and be victorious.

A sense of hope also is extremely important to success, as is faith in God and in oneself; as well as faith in the processes that are used to attain success. If the processes chosen are based on scriptural instruction, they are likely to be successful and easy to accomplish. Attempting to make it through this complex world without spiritual guidance is like trying to sustain oneself in the wilderness without basic provisions like food and water, hardly worth the attempt. Jesus has forged the path in the wilderness, taught others to navigate the treacherous wilderness of the world with pure conscience and to guide others on their quest for a closer relationship with God. Jesus is a link to the greatest power in the universe and He is a Shepherd who will not flee in the face of adversity.

While a hireling might run away when the wolf shows up snarling and ready to attack, Jesus stands the ground; and while He gives no clemency to enemies who will not repent, He is compassionate to those who do repent and call on Him for guidance. Those who repent and entrust their lives to Him are sure to find immediate and lasting benefits. He turns hearts and lives with power and authority, and He willingly stands as Advocate on behalf of all who trust in Him.

Live More Abundantly with Less Baggage

Jesus' promises provide insight into the stark contrast between the worldly and the heavenly, but He taught us how to live more abundantly in the present as we await eternal salvation. His desire for us to lead more fulfilling lives was seen in His teachings. He and His disciples, as fishers of men, were able to catch a generation of followers into the net of salvation. Those followers, in turn, brought more faithful ones into Jesus' sheepfold. Jesus turned the light on in a world of darkness, and the world has been changed so dramatically that even our calendars were recreated to count the days since He was with us in the flesh.

Amid a flurry of 'new' discoveries about Jesus, we must work to discern the truth about who He was, is, and ever will be. He worked so hard to create the corporate change that the world was so desperately in need of, that He poured out His very life. Afterward, His apostles did the same, good evidence that those who knew Him best were fully convinced of His Power and His Glory. They were rebuked, beaten, imprisoned, and even killed, all standing up for the principles of their faith in Him. They considered it an honor to suffer for Him. Today, it is still possible to have a personal relationship with Him, a complete mystery to those who do not understand grace through faith; but, to those who truly know Christ and carry Him in their hearts, the only mystery is why more people do not seek Him out. Those who are dedicated to Jesus will still suffer, because we are in the world, but they carry within them a hope so profound that they see through seeing eyes and hear with hearing ears, understanding that suffering is temporary. Jesus has turned drunks and drug addicts into clean living people. He has turned thieves and liars into honest individuals. He has turned harlots and prostitutes into people of honor. People whose businesses were failing have become successful. Those whose marriages were failing have been reconciled. Those whose children were running amuck have drawn their families back together. Those who have truly accepted Him into their hearts do not even desire their old way of life because the contrast is so stark.

No king, no priest, no judge in the history of the world, has ever turned so many lives around as Jesus has, and still does today. Jesus was the greatest corporate turnaround expert in history, often turning multitudes at a time to seek a relationship with God through Him, and He is still the greatest corporate turnaround expert in the present time. He is the True and Faithful Shepherd who died for His flock that He might live in their hearts forever, and He alone has the power to deliver the flock, spotless and blameless, to God in Heaven. *Indeed, Jesus Christ is the greatest corporate turnaround expert of all times.*

Key Learning Points:

o   Revitalization is a succession that follows the recovery phase to propel the corporation from a state of merely being functional to that of being a thriving, growing, and dynamic entity.
o   While no man has the power and authority of Christ to lay down such a broad foundation, it is possible to emulate the values He conveyed and to integrate those values into the way one conducts their business
o   If the ultimate objective is to live and work in a manner that is pleasing to God, the choices and actions made by individuals are more likely to be successful and well founded.
o   Another element fundamental to successful revitalization is the appropriate development of the staff.

- A healthy company will consume three meals a day, those being 'vision for breakfast, feedback for lunch, and action for dinner'.
- Furthering the effort by applying biblical principles enhances the likelihood of creating a healthy and thriving entity.
- To invoke the power to turn one's life around and ultimately to turn one's business to prosperity, there is only one major requirement, surrender. Surrender to the yoke of Jesus, which He said would be easy, and the burden would be light.

Conclusion

If your companies and businesses are sinking, you badly need a corporate turnaround with the help of the greatest turnaround expert, Jesus Christ. His values, teachings, and parables have created an impact when applied in our workplace. Successful testimonials have been presented by people upon adhering to Biblical principles in their businesses.

The first step in turnaround is to understand its pitfalls; consequences always go with compromises, but we also we need to be careful of that. After this, we need to define our purpose and goals, to have an amazingly fresh start. Being a servant leader is also very significant where it teaches us to be humble as what Jesus did with his ministry.

Having a fresh start requires starting with a clean slate, meaning being cautious in every deed you have done, for nothing is hidden from Him, everything will be unveiled in time. Also, starting with a clean slate involves seeking the right answers. Jesus, our turnaround expert has all the answers. He has the answers in governing ethically and morally, having a right master-servant relationship, and enhancing employer-employee relationship.

Finally, the key to achieving victory is surrender - surrendering to the goodness and faithfulness of our Lord and Savior, Jesus Christ, our corporate turnaround expert. A simple poem of God's faithfulness and goodness will be left for you to ponder on:

Jesus, the greatest turnaround expert

Whenever you face challenges
Which are difficult to overcome
When the path becomes narrow
And treading it is no fun
When life gets you down
And motivation is lost
When darkness surrounds you
And you feel that all is lost
Seek out Jesus,
The all in one expert
The greatest turnaround specialist
Through ages come
Use His teachings to elevate
And motivate at least some.

Let Jesus be the guide
For problems that you hide
Just abide by the rules
And follow Him in an even stride.
Find the inner strength,
And face up to challenges.
Never ever fear,
The Master,
Is always here,
Right besides you
Holding your hand
Ready to guide you!.
So, Now! Seek out Jesus,

Jesus, The only expert
The greatest turnaround specialist
Through ages come
Use His teachings to elevate
Escalate and get the power
To differentiate, and motivate
You, my friend
Into the correct trend.

Resources:

Price Waterhouse Coopers —
www.stevenage.gov.uk/.../dnld_executive_2/east_nh-nhstrust-update.pdf;internal&action=save.action

Gujarat Ambuja Cements Limited —
http://www.naukri.com/gpw/gac/index.htm

Kenyan Asians —
http://www.redhotcurry.com/archive/money/2004/pharma_families.htm

Thailand businesses —
http://www.ethicalcorp.com/content.asp?ContentID=1382

VinaPay —
http://www.vinapay.com.vn/?lang=en&page=aboutus
-

Aspect Software —
http://www.contactcenterworld.com/view/contact-center-news/Concerto-Software-And-Aspect-Communications-Complete-Merger.asp

Catholic Human Resource Executives —
http://findarticles.com/p/articles/mi_qa3859/is_200203/ai_n9048350

HKT-PCCW —
findarticles.com/p/articles/mi_m0WDQ/is_2000_August_7/ai_63946942

Nike—
http://www.thirdworldtraveler.com/Boycotts/Nike_Do
ntDoIt_GX.html

www.ingramcontent.com/pod-product-compliance
Lightning Source LLC
Chambersburg PA
CBHW062014200326
41519CB00017B/4795